Cooking with
LESS IRON

Cooking with
LESS IRON

Easy-to-Prepare, Reasonably Priced
Meals That Reduce the Amount
of Iron in Your Diet

CHERYL GARRISON

CUMBERLAND HOUSE PUBLISHING
NASHVILLE, TENNESSEE

A portion of the proceeds received from the sale of this book will be donated to Iron Disorders Institute.

Published by Cumberland House Publishing, Inc., 431 Harding Industrial Drive, Nashville, TN 37211

Cover design: Gore Studios, Inc.

Library of Congress Cataloging-in-Publication Data

Garrison, Cheryl
    Cooking with less iron : easy-to-prepare, reasonably priced meals that reduce the amount of iron in your diet / Cheryl Garrison.
      p. cm.
    Includes bibliographical references and index.
    ISBN 1-58182-223-5 (pbk. : alk. paper)
    1. Hemochromatosis—Diet therapy—Recipes. 2. Iron—Metabolism—Disorders—Diet therapy—Recipes.   I. Title.
    RC632.H4 G373 2001
      641.5'632—dc21

                                  2001047435

Printed in the United States of America
1 2 3 4 5 6 7 — 06 05 04 03 02 01

Cooking with Less Iron is dedicated to three women
who taught me about the benefits of good nutrition:
Naoma Goben, Elsa Blanton, and Irene Tate.

A special thanks to my husband Webb Garrison, my son David,
Kay Owen, Donna Duncan, Dr. Eugene Weinberg, Dr. Richard Passwater,
Dr. Janet Hunt, Dr. Mark Princell, Chris and Harry Kieffer,
Art Callahan, and Julie Pitkin.

Contents

FOREWORD

It's ironic! For decades in the United States, there has been an intensive education program urging people to eat foods rich in iron, mainly red meats. However, that is bad advice for the more than one million Americans who unknowingly have iron overload disorders—nor has there even been an education program to warn people of this deadly problem. Erroneously, most authorities still believe that iron overload disorders are rare. I don't believe that a deadly disease that affects more than a million Americans is rare.

Iron is vital for the transport and utilization of oxygen, so much so that it may be said that a partnership exists between the two that requires maintaining a balance. We often hear that iron deficiency can be a problem for about 10 percent of toddlers, teenage girls and women of childbearing age in the U.S., and for more than one billion people worldwide, according to official estimates. It's very common for nutritionists and physicians to recommend that people with poor or questionable diets take iron supplements without even testing for iron deficiency. However, few people realize that dietary iron is contraindicated for about 1 in every 250 Americans.

It's not that they eat too much iron, but that they have a genetic abnormality that causes "iron overload disorder." As many as 1 in 9 Americans carry one of the genes that can lead to the disorder. This makes it the most common known genetic disorder in the U.S. It is now believed that even having one of the two genes may, in some cases, lead to an iron absorption abnormality.

The problem is compounded by the fact that possibly between 1 million and 1.5 million Americans have undetected iron overload and do not become aware of their deadly disease until it is too late. The symptoms, such as fatigue and depression, are common to a number of ailments, which are, unfortunately, too often confusing, and physicians are taught that iron overload disorders are rare genetic diseases. Actually, as already mentioned, hereditary hemochromatosis is the most commonly inherited disease. Because most physicians still believe that iron overload disorders are rare, one-third of hereditary hemochromatosis (the worst form of iron overload) patients in one study reported that they had to see an average of eleven physicians before they were correctly diagnosed, and one-fifth reported that this process took ten years.

Fortunately, *Cooking with Less Iron* helps clarify the problem. It provides an easy-to-understand explanation of the science behind the iron overload disorders and presents practical and expert advice on how to deal with iron overload disorders. The more than two hundred recipes in this book can become part of a dietary plan and help the more than one million Americans having iron overload disorders.

—Richard Passwater, Ph.D., Director,
Solgar Nutritional Research Center,
Berlin, Maryland, and Vice President of Research,
Solgar Vitamin & Herb Co., Inc.

INTRODUCTION

As a physician it is rewarding when a diagnosis can be accompanied by hope. Such is the case with early detection of hereditary hemochromatosis, a leading cause of iron overload disease.

Hereditary hemochromatosis (HHC) is a genetic disorder of iron metabolism. It is not a blood disease. A person cannot catch hemochromatosis; it is inherited from their parents. Persons with HHC have a defect somewhere in the absorption process. This causes them to take in excessive amounts of iron from their diet. Iron cannot be excreted, and after several years time this excess iron accumulates in vital organs such as the liver, heart, pancreas, joints, and brain. Iron-loaded organs cannot function properly and the result can be disease, such as diabetes, liver disease, arthritis, depression, impotence, infertility, or premature death from a heart attack.

When detected early, HHC can be treated and dramatically reduce a person's risk of developing these serious and chronic diseases. Hemochromatosis is a condition we physicians can do something about. We can suspect it in anyone because it is common: 1 in 250 Americans are believed to have genetic hemochromatosis; nearly 30 million are believed to be carriers. Physicians can suspect HHC in anyone with a history of chronic disease, especially when a parent has died prematurely. Doctors can identify it early because it's real; with the discovery of *HFE,* the gene for hemochromatosis, the condition, once thought to be rare, was validated as real and prevalent among Caucasians. Also, HHC is easily detected. Two simple blood tests, serum ferritin and transferrin iron saturation percentage, can reveal elevated tissue iron levels. Physicians can also use genetic analysis to detect HHC, especially in families where one case has been diagnosed. Doctors should inform families about HHC because it can kill. Undetected and untreated hemochromatosis is one of the greatest risk factors for chronic disease, which can lead to death at an early age. The mean age of death from heart attack in undiagnosed males with hemochromatosis is estimated to be age fifty-eight; for females it is believed to be age seventy-four.

When I diagnosed my first case of hereditary hemochromatosis there was very little information about the disorder. Except for treatment using aggressive phlebotomy there was nothing to help a physician guide a patient in the management of their iron imbalance. Diet guidelines were nonexistent or too extreme. Through organizations such as the Iron Disorders Institute and its educational publications, we now have more to offer patients with HHC. We have learned about the problems associated with over-bleeding, how to determine reaccumulation patterns, that tobacco smoke is loaded with iron, and that certain foods inhibit or enhance the absorption of dietary iron. With this knowledge, it is clear there are preventive measures that can help control the absorption of the metal. This information can be vital to a person with iron loading disorder such as hemochromatosis.

Careful monitoring while deironing, especially during the final phase, compliance with therapy, and controlling one's diet, are key to managing hemochromatosis. In *Cooking with Less Iron* Cheryl Garrison has combined her years of experience as an educator, her knowledge about iron imbalances, and her practical experiences as a restaurant owner to create a simple and helpful eating plan for persons with HHC. Anyone with excessive tissue iron can benefit from the recipes and helpful tips in this book.

Talk with your physician about hereditary hemochromatosis. Contact the Iron Disorders Institute for literature about the disorder and visit their website at www.irondisorders.org. Meanwhile, keep your iron levels in balance, eat right, kick the tobacco habit, and enjoy life!

—*Mark Princell, M.D.,*
St. Francis Health System,
Greenville, South Carolina
Iron Disorders Institute Scientific Advisory
Board Member

WHY COOK WITH LESS IRON?

Individuals with hereditary hemochromatosis absorb abnormally high amounts of iron from their diet. Iron cannot be excreted and, over time, the metal accumulates to toxic levels in vital organs such as the liver, heart, brain, and joints. Persons with high iron levels are at an increased risk for premature heart attack, diabetes, arthritis, liver disease, depression, and hormone imbalances resulting in loss of sex drive, infertility, or impotence. Controlling one's intake and absorption of iron can lower the risk of developing chronic disease and experiencing premature death.

Iron is an essential nutrient; human beings could not survive without it, but excesses of the metal can be fatal. People can enjoy the best health when all nutrients are in balance and adequate amounts are available for normal body function without creating harmful excesses.

For hundreds of years the focus has been on iron deficiencies, which remain a critical health issue. Another critical health issue involving iron is excessive levels of the metal. Only recently have clinicians begun to realize the health risks associated with too much iron and the consequences of late detection and absence of treatment for iron loading conditions such as hereditary hemochromatosis.

Radiologists trained in the use of specialized magnetic resonance imaging (MRI), have observed high levels of iron in the brains of patients who have Alzheimer's, early onset Parkinson's, Huntington's disease, schizophrenia, bipolar disease, and epilepsy.

A fairly common bacterium, *Vibrio vulnificus*, which is not harmful to people with normal iron levels, can be deadly to a person with excess tissue iron. Exposure to this bacterium, which is found in raw shellfish such as oysters, has caused the deaths of persons with high iron levels.

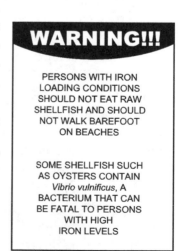

WARNING!!!

PERSONS WITH IRON LOADING CONDITIONS SHOULD NOT EAT RAW SHELLFISH AND SHOULD NOT WALK BAREFOOT ON BEACHES

SOME SHELLFISH SUCH AS OYSTERS CONTAIN *Vibrio vulnificus*, A BACTERIUM THAT CAN BE FATAL TO PERSONS WITH HIGH IRON LEVELS

Persons who are at high risk for cancer can benefit from maintaining low normal iron levels. Cancer cells require iron to replicate. By beginning early reduction of dietary iron and avoiding supplemental iron, a person can provide some level of prevention against the disease.

Many patients with an inflammatory disease such as arthritis, infections such as viral hepatitis or AIDS, and some cancer patients may have improved responses to treatment when iron levels are reduced.

Reprinted with permission from Iron Disorders Institute, 2000

Important Ferritin Reference Ranges		
ferritin	Adult Males	Adult Females
Normal Range	up to 300ng/mL	up to 200ng/mL
In treatment*	below 100ng/mL	below 100ng/mL
Ideal maintenance	25-75ng/mL	25-75ng/mL
Adolescents, Juveniles, Infants & Newborns of normal height and weight for their age and gender		
Male ages 10-19 23-70ng/mL	Infants 7-12 months	60-80ng/mL
Female ages 10-19 6-40ng/mL	Newborn 1-6 months	6-41ng/mL
Children ages 6-9 10-55ng/mL	Newborn 1-30 days	6-400ng/mL
Children ages 1-5 6-24ng/mL		

Chart reprinted with permission from Iron Disorders Institute, 2000

How do I know if I have iron overload? Hemoglobin values can help a physician determine the presence of anemia, or an overproduction of red blood cells, but hemoglobin cannot determine the presence of excess tissue iron. Two tests that can help determine tissue iron levels are serum ferritin and transferrin iron saturation percentage. These tests are best done fasting, that is, nothing by mouth except water after midnight or prior to bloodwork. Normal range for saturation percentage is 25 to 35 percent. Normal ranges for ferritin differ with age and gender.

Can a person have both anemia and iron overload? Yes. Persons who have certain iron loading conditions such as G6PD (glucose-6 phosphate dehydrogenase enzyme deficiency), sideroblastic anemia, thalassemia, and those who are transfusion-dependent will develop acquired iron overload if the excess iron contained in whole-blood transfusions is not removed. This is done clinically using a prescribed agent such as Desferal. A condition called anemia of chronic disease often fools physicians into diagnosing iron deficiency anemia and recommending iron supplementation. In fact these people are actually exhibiting a natural defense mechanism called the iron withholding defense system, identified in the late 1970s by Indiana University professor of microbiology Dr. Eugene Weinberg. In an attempt to withhold excess iron from harmful pathogens, this system is activated in humans whenever an infection, inflammation, or early stages of tumor development are present. Individuals with anemia of chronic disease can experience a slight drop in hemoglobin and a rise in serum ferritin. This type of anemia corrects itself when the underlying disease such as infection, inflammation, or tumor is treated and no longer present.

How do humans regulate absorption of iron? Humans with normal metabolism have the ability to regulate absorption of nutrients such as iron. In times of high need for iron, the body adjusts to take in more of the metal. Some people do not have the benefit of this natural regulatory mechanism. Persons with inherited disorders of iron metabolism such as hemochromatosis and those who are at risk of iron overload with sideroblastic anemia, thalassemia, sickle-cell anemia, G6PD deficiency, or chronic disease and are transfusion-dependent must take steps to reduce the amount of iron acquired or absorbed. For those with normal hemoglobin levels such as hereditary hemochromatosis, blood donation or therapeutic phlebotomy is used to reduce iron levels. For those with subnormal hemoglobin values, iron chelation therapy is currently the only way to safely and efficiently remove excess iron.

What are the types of iron we consume? Humans consume two types of iron: heme iron and nonheme iron.

Heme iron is derived from organic sources such as the blood proteins, hemoglobin, and myoglobin contained in meat. This type of iron is in a form more easily absorbed by the body. About 10 percent or less of dietary iron consumed in American diets is heme iron, even though meat consumption in the U.S. is high. For persons with normal iron metabolism only 20 to 25 percent of the heme iron consumed is actually absorbed. For example, a four-ounce hamburger contains about 3 milligrams of iron; about 1.2 milligrams are heme and about 1.8 milligrams are non-heme. The amount of heme iron absorbed from that four-ounce hamburger would be approximately a third of a milligram. Persons with abnormal iron metabolism

IRON	per 3.2 oz serving MEAT		
	total iron MILLIGRAMS	heme iron percentage of total iron	heme iron MILLIGRAMS
VENISON	4.5	51	2.3
LAMB	3.1	55	1.7
BEEF			
RUMP STEAK	2.9	52	1.5
SIRLOIN STEAK	2.5	52	1.3
ROUND STEAK	3.2	50	1.6
TOP ROUND	2.5	48	1.2
GROUND	2.5	40	1.0
BRISKET	2.0	25	0.5
VEAL	1.9	40*	0.7*
PORK	1.3	23	0.3
PROCESSED MEATS			
SAUSAGE (VEAL)	0.7	40*	0.2*
BOILED HAM	0.7	40*	0.2*
LIVER PATE	5.0	16	0.8
CHICKEN	0.6	40*	0.2*
FISH			
COD	0.2	0.0	0.0
MACKEREL	0.7	0.0	0.0
SALMON	0.6	17	0.1
MUSSELS	4.6	48	2.2
LOBSTER	1.6	40*	0.6*
SHRIMP	2.6	40*	1.0*
* resources vary			

such as hereditary hemochromatosis can absorb up to four times the iron as a person with normal metabolism. Therefore, 80 to 100 percent of heme iron can be absorbed, or approximately 1.2 milligrams from the same four-ounce hamburger. Calcium is the only substance that has been found to inhibit heme iron, while numerous substances can inhibit the absorption of nonheme iron. Though there are foods that will impede or enhance absorption of nonheme iron, absorption of heme iron is little affected by these foods.

Nonheme iron: About 40 to 45 percent of the iron contained in meat is heme, the other 55 to 60 percent is nonheme. Iron contained in plants is almost entirely nonheme iron, though plants do contain minute traces of heme iron. Nonheme iron represents the majority of dietary iron humans consume. This type of iron is inorganic and is derived from grains, nuts, fruits, vegetables, fortificants, or contaminant iron such as that derived from water, soil or cooking untensils. Unlike heme iron, the iron from all these sources must be changed before absorption can take place.

What changes iron so that it can be absorbed? When nonheme iron is ingested it is in a form called ferric iron. Ferric iron cannot be absorbed by humans; it mixes with stomach acid (hydrochloric acid) and is changed into ferrous iron. Ferrous iron is the form of iron that can be absorbed; it moves out of the stomach into the first part of the intestine called the duodenum. This is the point at which scientists believe the majority of absorption takes place. Some scientists speculate that there is another absorption site farther down in the intestinal tract where minute amounts of iron can be absorbed, but this theory is still being researched. Certain substances can interfere with the absorption of iron; knowing what these are and avoiding or including these substances with main meals can help an individual control dietary iron absorption.

Can diet reduce stored iron levels? Not for a person with serious iron overload; only blood loss will efficiently lower iron levels. A dietary plan can significantly reduce absorption of iron from the diet and therefore reduce the stored iron in ferritin. Reduced absorption can lower the number of therapeutic phlebotomies needed for many with hemochromatosis-related iron overload. One can induce iron deficiency anemia with a specialized diet, such as a strict vegetarian diet. These individuals usually do not have excess iron stores, though there are rare exceptions. Also, taking a daily aspirin and vigorous exercise can cause minute amounts of intestinal blood loss. These measures can contribute to tissue iron reduction but are considered preventive measures more than therapeutic approaches.

Is there a pill that will reduce iron levels? Yes, but it is not for persons with hemochromatosis unless they are also anemic. A pill called Ferriprox was approved in Europe for persons with thalassemia who could not tolerate Desferal, a chemical given intravenously that removes iron. Both drugs are used to treat persons with concurrent iron overload and anemia. Desferal is expensive and removes only about 50 milligrams in twelve hours. One phlebotomy takes about twenty minutes and removes about 250 milligrams each time! As long as a person's hemoglobin remains sufficient for phlebotomy or blood donation, this method is the safest and most efficient way to remove tissue iron.

What is the best diet plan for someone with an iron loading condition? No single food or substance is a cure-all; balance is the key. A good diet plan for anyone, including someone with an iron imbalance needs to be simple and incorporate all food groups. It also needs to be easy to follow and adhere to, and it needs to be dynamic, changing, as the individual's needs change. Take for example the tomato, which is rich in vitamin C and beta carotene. Vitamin C can be destroyed with cooking but not beta carotene. However, foods like tomatoes should not be eliminated from one's diet just because of these qualities. With the exception of organ meats or raw shellfish, *Cooking with Less Iron* teaches a person simple techniques that allow for all foods to be consumed.

Every person is different. A person with iron overload doesn't fit neatly into a single patient profile. Some people have elevated serum ferritin with only slightly elevated transferrin iron saturation percentages. These individuals may need only a few phlebotomies and minor diet changes. Some persons have extremely high iron levels and need long-term aggressive phlebotomy. Some are smokers and consume alcohol, two dangerous practices, especially in the presence of excessive iron. These individuals might need a strict diet and an aggressive therapeutic phlebotomy regimen. Others may be totally deironed and just want to maintain healthy iron levels by controlling absorption of the metal. Recipes in *Cooking with Less Iron* are designed with all of these individual needs in mind. People just diagnosed and who have very high tissue iron levels may want to plan the majority of meals from this book and follow the eating plan closely. Persons who are deironed and want to minimize the amount of iron absorbed might select recipes from this book two or three times a week.

The *Cooking with Less Iron* eating plan allows for flexibility with its suggested substitutions and provides for reward meals, such as a beef entrée once a week. With the exception of supplemental iron, no nutrient or food group is eliminated from the daily diet. Measures to reduce the amount of iron absorbed are incorporated into the eating plan. Recipes in *Cooking with Less Iron* were taste-tested and selected for their universal appeal regardless of age or gender. Also, because substances that inhibit the absorption of iron also inhibit absorption of other nutrients, this eating plan includes nutrient supplementation by taking a daily vitamin supplement.

What about supplementation? When a person consumes substances that can inhibit the absorption of iron, those same substances inhibit the absorption of other nutrients such as zinc and copper. Taking a good daily multivitamin is one way to assure that other nutrients blocked from absorption are replenished through supplementation. A good once-a-day multiple vitamin with minerals excluding iron is likely sufficient for any adult with an iron loading disorder. Solgar makes several iron-free daily multivitamins: Omnium Iron Free and Iron Free Formula VM-75 are two that might be considered. CVS Drugs makes a good daily multiple sold as Spectravite™ without iron. An excellent daily vitamin is One Daily Iron Free™ a product of

MegaFoods, which can be found in health food stores. Some daily supplements require a person to take six to eight pills a day. Not only can this be expensive, but one might actually experience gastrointestinal discomfort as a result of high doses of supplements. When looking for a daily vitamin supplement, find one where "one dose" is obtained from one pill, as is the case with the vitamins recommended above.

In recent decades, scientists have found ways that are more sensitive in detecting the effects of substances on the absorption of iron including nutrients such as beta carotene, zinc, copper and calcium. Dr. Raymond Glahn, of the Cornell University Agricultural Research Division of the USDA, developed an artificial gut that provides for better accuracy in establishing bioavailability of iron from the diet. "Bioavailability" is the extent to which a nutrient or drug is accessible to the body for its intended use. According to Dr. Janet Hunt of the Agricultural Research Team, Grand Forks Human Nutrition Research Center, "Iron absorption from food can vary up to tenfold depending on the bioavailability of iron." Prior to modern inventions such as the artificial gut and breakthroughs in genetics, scientists had few methods for determining iron absorption with such precision. Dr. Miguel Layrisse, a world-renowned expert in absorption, provides a brief description of how science has studied absorption:

> In the '40s iron absorption was determined by chemistry. The amount of iron absorbed was calculated as the difference between dietary iron and excreted iron. The other method used to measure dietary iron was hemoglobin repletion. In the '70s the measurement of plasma ferritin was an important contribution to iron metabolism to assess iron deficiency and iron overload. In the same decade the extrinsic and intrinsic labeled methodology was an important advancement. The '70s and '80s were years where scientists aimed at finding iron absorption inhibitors, namely coffee, calcium, tea, zinc, and fiber. The '80s and '90s were characterized by the emerging knowledge of iron absorption from a food, a meal, and a complete diet and for the favorable effect of food iron fortification in developing countries. Also, the effect of iron excess in overall health and myocardial infarction in developed countries was studied."
>
> Dr. Miguel Layrisse, Centro de Medicina Experimental, Instituto Venezolano de Investigaciones Cientificas Center for Experimental Medicine and Institute for Scientific Investigations, University of Central Venezuela

What foods increase or inhibit absorption of iron? (See the chart at right.)

Substances that increase iron absorption:

Ascorbic acid, or vitamin C, occurs naturally in vegetables and fruits, especially citrus; it can also be synthesized for use in supplements. Ascorbic acid enhances the absorption of nutrients such as iron. One glass of orange juice (about 100 milligrams of vitamin C) can counteract the inhibiting effect of a cup of tea. Studies suggest that greater than or equal to 50 mg of ascorbic acid would be required to overcome the inhibitory effects on iron absorption of any meal containing greater than 100 mg of tannic acid. In studies concerning the effects of ascorbic acid on iron absorption, 100 milligrams of ascorbic acid increased iron absorption from a specific meal by 4.14 times. In a standard meal of meat, potatoes, and milk, 100 milligrams (mg) of ascorbic acid increased absorption of iron by 67 percent. The addition of 100 mg of ascorbic acid to a specially formulated liquid meal containing 85 mg of phytate increased absorption by 3.14 times.

Alcohol enhances absorption of iron and contributes to liver disease. Limiting alcohol consumption to social events, special occasions such as dining out, or celebrations may help a person reduce the amount consumed. Studies show that heavy drinkers have high iron levels. Approximately 20 to 30 percent of those who are heavy consumers of alcohol acquire up to twice the amount of dietary iron as do moderate or light drinkers. Alcohol will hasten liver disease such as cirrhosis. Patients who have developed cirrhosis increase their chance of developing liver cancer by 200-fold. Alcohol in the presence of high iron can also cause brain damage. Brain cells of alcohol-induced lab rats were found to contain an alarming amount of "free iron." A "standard drink" is defined as 13.5 grams of alcohol: 12 ounces of beer, 5 ounces of wine, 1.5 ounces distilled spirits. "Moderate consumption" is defined as

absorption of IRON

substances that enhance absorption

- ascorbic acid vitamin C
- alcohol
- beta-carotene
- meat, some fish/seafood
- EDTA+ fe
- Ferrochel
- hydrochloric acid

substances that inhibit absorption

- polyphenols: (good sources)
  - tannins (coffee, tea, red wine)
  - chlorogenic acid (cocoa)
  - phenolic acid (apples)
- excessive iron* or zinc supplementation
- oxalates (spinach, oregano)
- eggs
- phytates (high fiber foods)
- phosphates in dairy
- calcium

*from studies related to iron deficiency anemia

Reprinted with permission from Iron Disorders Institute, 2000

WARNING!!!

Grapefruit juice can cause serious and dangerous side effects, including fatalities, when taken with certain medications. Something in the fruit causes drug potency to be increased up to twelve fold.

two drinks per day for an adult male; one drink per day for females or those older than 65 regardless of gender. Options to consider might be nonalcoholic or low alcohol content beer and wine. Though red wine is reported to be healthy for the heart, it is likely the polyphenol content in red wine that is providing the greater benefit. Except for the sedating quality of alcohol, a handful of red grapes will provide equal, if not greater health benefits.

Beta-Carotene is one of more than 100 carotenoids that occur naturally in plants and animals. Carotenoids are yellow to red pigments that are contained in foods such as apricots, beets and beet greens, carrots, collard greens, corn, red grapes, oranges, peaches, prunes, red peppers, spinach, sweet potatoes, tomatoes, turnip greens and yellow squash. Beta carotene enables the body to produce vitamin A. In studies of the effects of vitamin A and beta carotene on absorption of iron, vitamin A did not significantly increase iron absorption under the experimental conditions employed. However, beta carotene significantly increased absorption of the metal. Moreover, in the presence of phytates or tannic acid, beta carotene generally overcame the inhibitory effects of both compounds depending on their concentrations. Like vitamin E, beta carotene is an excellent antioxidant.

FOODS HIGH IN BETA-CAROTENE

microgram/100 grams edible portion

Apricots	2,554
Asparagus	493
Beets	2,560
Broccoli	1,042
Brussels sprouts	465
Butter with salt	158
Carrots	8,836
Chard	3,954
Cilantro	3,440
Collards	4,418
Endive	960
Grape leaves (canned)	2,838
Grapefruit (pink)	603
Kale (cooked)	6,202
Lettuce (Romaine)	1,272
Lettuce (iceberg)	192
Mangos (fresh)	445
Margarine spread	721
Melon (cantaloupe)	1,595
Okra	170
Orange (fresh)	122
Papayas (fresh)	276
Peaches (fresh)	97
Peas	320
Peppers green	22
Peppers red	2,220
Peppers yellow	120
Spinach (cooked)	5,242
Spinach (raw)	5,597
Squash (yellow)	90
Squash (zucchini)	410
Sweet potato	9,488
Tomatoes (paste)	1,242
Tomatoes fresh	393

Beta-Carotene is one of the carotenoids, which are the the the red, green, yelow and orange pigments found in fruits and vegetables. Beta-Carotene enables the body to produce vitamin A and is highly effective as an anti-oxidant.

This important nutrient should not be eliminated from the diet because of the health benefits it provides. Take caution to drink tea with meals high in beta-Carotene to further inhibit absorption of iron

chart created from carotenoid values database USDA

EDTA+fe and Ferrochel are additive iron compounds and are emerging as candidates for fortification by major food manufacturers. Individuals with conditions such as hemochromatosis who are at high risk for iron overload will need to avoid food products fortified with these two compounds. Both additives were found to exceed absorption capabilities of the commonly used fortificant ferrous sulfate.

Ferrochel is an iron bis-glycine chelate. Glycine is a nonessential amino acid used as a chelate. This chelate has a 2:1 ratio to the mineral, hence, "bis," meaning "two," glycines to one iron atom. Albion Laboratories, Salt Lake City,

Utah, owns the patent rights to produce this type of chelate, which is much more effective at delivering a high bioavailable form of iron than ferrous sulfate.

Fe-EDTA is a compound of iron salts and EDTA (ethylenediaminetetraacetic acid), a broad-spectrum chelate, which means it binds with many minerals. It too performed well in the same absorption studies. Both EDTA and bis-glycine–chelated iron were absorbed at the rate of two to three times that of ferrous sulfate. When combined with phytase, the enzyme that breaks down phytates in fiber, Ferrochel and EDTA increase the bioavailability of iron even more.

Phytase is the enzyme that breaks down phytate, a compound found in fiber and an inhibitor of iron absorption. Phytase is sometimes added to foods to increase absorption of iron.

Hydrochloric acid is the acid found in the stomach that breaks down food and makes it available for absorption. Coffee can increase production of stomach acid, even though coffee is also a known inhibitor of iron due to its tannin and chlorogenic acid content.

Meat, especially red meat, increases the absorption of nonheme iron. Meat contains heme but it also contains animal fats, which can increase absorption of nonheme iron. It has been calculated that 1 gram of meat (about 20 percent protein) has an enhancing effect on nonheme iron absorption equivalent to that of 1 milligram of ascorbic acid. A Latin American–type meal (maize, rice, and black beans) with a low iron bioavailability had the same improved bioavailability when either 75 g of meat or 50 mg of ascorbic acid were added.

Substances that inhibit absorption of iron:

Polyphenols are phenolic compounds, such as chlorogenic acid found in cocoa, coffee, and some herbs. Phenolic acid found in apples, peppermint, and some herbal teas, and tannins found in black teas, coffee, cocoa, spices, walnuts, fruits such as apples, blackberries, raspberries, and blueberries all contain polyphenols. One must remember however, that some of these foods also contain vitamin C and beta carotene. Of the polyphenols, Swedish cocoa and certain teas demonstrate the most powerful iron absorption inhibiting capabilities, in some cases up to 90 percent. Coffee is high in tannin and chlorogenic acid; one cup of certain types of coffee can inhibit iron absorption by as much as 60 percent.

Phytate is a compound contained in soy protein and fiber found in walnuts, almonds, sesame seeds, dried beans, lentils and peas, cereals, and whole grains. Recent absorption studies in humans have demonstrated that even low levels of phytate (about 5 percent of the amounts in cereal whole flours) have a strong inhibitory effect on iron absorption. Phytate levels are reduced during yeast fermentation in rye, white, and whole-wheat breads, and sourdough leavening results in an almost complete degradation of phytate.

Phosphates are compounds used to whiten food products; they are found in modified tapioca starch, bacon, toothpaste, certain medications, and some dairy products. The ability of phosphates to inhibit the absorption of iron is not completely understood.

Calcium is an essential mineral; it is found in foods such as milk, yogurt, cheese, sardines, canned salmon, tofu, broccoli, almonds, figs, turnip greens, and rhubarb. The iron inhibitory capability of calcium has long been a debated issue. Studies that indicate calcium can impair the absorption of iron have been confirmed by the USDA Agricultural Research Department. Indeed, calcium can inhibit the absorption of heme iron. Where 50 milligrams or less of calcium had no effect on absorption, calcium in amounts of 300 to 600 milligrams inhibited the absorption of heme iron similarly to nonheme iron. One cup of skim milk contains about 300 milligrams of calcium.

Oxalates are compounds derived from oxalic acid and found in foods such as spinach, kale, beets, nuts, chocolate, tea, wheat bran, rhubarb, strawberries, and herbs such as oregano, basil, and parsley. Oxalates impair the absorption of nonheme iron. The presence of oxalates in spinach explains why the iron in spinach is not absorbed.

Eggs. The component in eggs that impairs absorption of iron may be due to a phosphoprotein called phosvitin. The binding capacity of this protein with iron may be responsible for the low bioavailability of iron from eggs and possibly the iron inhibiting ability of eggs called the "egg factor." The egg factor has been observed in several separate studies. One boiled egg can reduce absorption of iron in a meal by as much as 28 percent

Zinc is an essential mineral found in meat, eggs, seafood, and to

Although more iron is absorbed from larger doses of iron, the percentage absorbed decreases as the amount of the dose increases.

Supplimental Iron (milligrams)

100 mgs — 10% or 1 milligram
10 mgs — 15% >1.5 milligrams
1 mg — 25% >1/4 milligram

Percentage of Iron Absorbed (%)

Reprinted with permission from Iron Disorders Institute, 2000

some degree in grains. High doses of supplemental zinc can interfere with copper utilization, which can lead to impaired metabolism of iron. It should also be noted that for persons with normal metabolism, high doses of supplemental iron can also reduce the amount of iron absorbed by the body.

Fats. When we think of fat, images of oozing butter, greasy potato chips, and thick juicy steaks might come to mind. Fat-free diets continue to be followed faithfully by people still under the false impression that all fat is bad. Recent research indicates that certain fats actually lower the bad type of cholesterol, reduce triglycerides, and lower blood pressure.

Fats are either saturated or unsaturated. Saturated fats are derived from both plant and animal sources and have been shown to promote plaque formation by raising blood cholesterol in animals and humans. Saturated fats are solid at room temperature and are derived from animal sources. Examples of saturated fats include chicken fat, bacon or lard, beef fat, butter, milk, cream, and cheese. Saturated-fat animal fats clog arteries and can elevate bad cholesterol, triglycerides, and blood pressure.

Trans unsaturated fats can also be formed from vegetable oil by the chemical process know as hydrogenation. Vegetable shortening, palm kernel oil, and coconut oil or the addition of hydrogen atoms to an unsaturated fat have been shown to increase the risk of heart disease. Hydrogenation gives foods, such as crackers, cookies, potato chips, French fries, and doughnuts, a longer shelf life by making them less likely to turn rancid. There is presently no way to determine the amount of trans unsaturated fats Americans are consuming since the revised food labels do not specify the amount contained in the product.

Bad fats can be catalysts for chemical reactions in the body that cause free radical activity. Free radicals contribute to degenerative disease and hasten the aging process. Iron can provide the oxygen that fat needs to set off this chemical reaction. A rotting apple or the rust on an automobile is an example of oxygen + iron free-radical activity. Eat sparingly of these types of fat; avoid or substitute when possible.

Unsaturated fats are liquid at room temperature. There are two types of unsaturated fats: polyunsaturated and monounsaturated. Within the polyunsaturated fats are yet another two types: Omega 6 and Omega 3 polyunsaturated fatty acids. One can be dangerous to our health; the other beneficial.

Polyunsaturated fatty acids (PUFA): Omega-6 PUFAs are derived from vegetable oils and are liquid at room temperature. They include corn, sunflower, safflower, soybean, and sesame oils. Salad dressing, margarine, and mayonnaise containing these oils are therefore high in polyunsaturated fat; eat these sparingly.

Omega-3 PUFA, found primarily in fish, is a good type of polyunsaturated fat. Omega-3 polyunsaturated fats do not increase serum cholesterol or LDL levels. Their effects are shown to lower the risk of cardiovascular disease and breast cancer. For persons concerned about iron in fish, the type of iron in most fish is primarily non-heme iron. Certain food substances such as tannin, fiber and dairy can inhibit the absorption of this type of iron. Fish, therefore, is an excellent protein choice and should be included in one's diet at least three to four times a week.

Other good fats: Monounsaturated fats are derived from plant sources. High amounts are found in olive, canola (rapeseed), and peanut oil, as well as avocados and certain nuts. Monounsaturated fats do not increase serum cholesterol or LDL levels. Their effects are shown to lower the risk of cardiovascular disease and breast cancer.

COOKING WITH LESS IRON EATING PLAN

Humans need nutrients such as fats, carbohydrates, protein, vitamins, minerals including iron, and adequate amounts of water to assure proper metabolism and optimal health. All foods contain some nutrients the body can utilize. Choosing the best source of a nutrient and eating those foods in balance and moderation is the key to enjoying a wide variety of tastes, including desserts. With the exception of foods to which one is allergic, persons with metabolic disorders can modify their diets to incorporate all foods.

Individuals with hemochromatosis (HHC) will want to reduce the amount of heme iron consumed and to incorporate foods that impede absorption of nonheme iron. These people still need iron for body function; they just need less of it in their diet because of their faulty iron regulatory mechanism. People with HHC have the ability to absorb quadruple the iron that a person with normal metabolism absorbs.

The *Cooking with Less Iron* eating plan is formulated for persons with conditions of iron overload such as hereditary hemochromatosis. Recipes are balanced for the

Cooking With Less Iron
EATING PLAN CHECKLIST

Use your menu planner spread sheet

- Plan ahead: decide your menu a week at a time
- Note the heme and nonheme content of foods
- Note Vitamin C content of foods to be eaten raw
- Note foods high in beta-carotene
- Plan Vitamin C or beta-carotene-rich foods as snacks
- Incorporate substances that inhibit iron absorption
- Avoid foods that enhance iron absorption at main meals
- Cook in glassware whenever possible
- Don't forget your daily vitamin
- Limit alcohol consumption
- Don't smoke or chew tobacco products
- Drink plenty of water
- Plan some daily exercise approved by your physician: walking, dancing, yoga, etc.
- Report any symptoms or changes to your physician

majority of persons who incorporate some physical activity into their daily routine, and do not smoke or drink excessively.

Any eating plan must be adjusted to meet the individual needs of persons with chronic conditions. Persons with arthritis, diabetes, heart disease, liver disease, cancer, or who are overweight or in chronic pain will want to adjust recipes for best results. Variety is key; any food might be tolerated occasionally but *occasionally* must be defined. For some, the word *occasionally* might mean every three days, once a week, once a month, etc. Discuss diet with your physician to determine how often exceptions to a prescribed diet may occur.

- Know the content of both nonheme and heme iron; use the food composition charts and the blank worksheets provided to calculate the amount of iron in foods you intend to use in your weekly meal plans.

- Incorporate into your menus foods that impair absorption of iron: tea, coffee, dairy, fiber.

- Avoid foods that enhance absorption of iron at mealtime: foods rich in vitamin C, beta carotene, or drinking alcohol. *Note:* Cooking destroys vitamin C.

- Eat vitamin C and beta carotene rich foods as snacks.

- Take daily vitamin supplements with snacks rather than with main meals.

- Use olive oil, which is high in monounsaturated fatty acids, a type of fat that contributes to prevention of chronic diseases such as cancer and heart trouble.

- Cook in glassware or ceramic ware such as Pyrex or Corningware when possible; especially avoid cooking in cast-iron skillets or on grills.

- Avoid grilled foods at restaurants except occasionally.

- Be compliant with therapeutic phlebotomies. No diet can replace this important aspect of therapy for those with iron overload.

- Drink plenty of water, at least a quart a day. Your body can get some water from foods, but most people tend not to eat adequate amounts of foods with high water content such as fruits and vegetables. Adequate hydration reduces the time it takes to remove a pint of blood.

- Don't smoke or chew tobacco products. Tobacco contains high amounts of iron. Inhalation of tobacco smoke can increase your risk of lung cancer. When foods or food products containing iron are eaten, the amount of iron absorbed from these foods is regulated in the intestine. When iron is inhaled, it bypasses this regulatory step, thus, iron contained in the tobacco smoke goes directly into the lungs. Also, any opportunity to impede absorption of iron by consuming foods such as tea or fiber is lost. Inhaled iron collects in lung cells called alveolar macrophages. These are the cells that help fight against infections and cancers in the lungs. When heavily burdened with iron, these cells cannot protect a person against opportunistic disease such as Legionnaires' pneumonia. Also, cancer cells thrive on iron. Mainstream tobacco smoke is estimated to contain as much as 0.1 percent of the metal contaminant; that is, 60,000 picograms of iron per cigarette smoked. Thus a one-pack/day smoker could inhale over one million picograms iron/day. In a number of reports, alveolar macrophages of smokers have been found to be brimming with iron—in many cases, in amounts sufficient to prevent the alveolar macrophages from killing cancer cells and pathogenic microbes.

- Plan ahead. Deciding what meals will be consumed during a week helps in several ways: This measure saves money and helps reduce the number of impulsive decisions to eat what is handy. Often these choices include fast food or foods that should be eaten on a limited basis. Planning ahead offers opportunities for reward meals such as an occasional lean cut of steak or a glass of red wine. Use the menu planner referring to the sample week of menus as a guideline. Leave the shopping list in a convenient place so that as certain foods are depleted these can be noted for the next trip to the grocery store.

A Note About Cookware

While a person is in the de-ironing process, the choice of cookware is important. Iron filings can get into the food, especially when cooking with cast-iron skillets, using a grill, or in some cases stainless steel cookware. The recommended choice is glassware such as Pyrex or ceramic ware such as Corning Ware. Once a person is de-ironed, occasional use of cast iron or stainless is fine. You will note that most recipes call for a stockpot, saucepan, or skillet. Depending on your iron status, choose the appropriate cookware.

All charts reprinted with permission from Iron Disorders Institute, 2000

Cooking with Less Iron Menu Planner

some serving sizes appear with recipes
* sauces can be omitted for lower calorie meal

	day one	day two	day three	day four	day five	day six	day seven
breakfast	2-egg western omelet / 1/2 cup blueberries / red potato homefries / coffee	3/4 cup Kellogg brand Complete Oat Bran cereal / 1/2 banana (not overripe) / 1/2 cup low-fat milk / coffee	bran muffin with walnuts / Neufchatel cheese / 1 medium pear / coffee	scrambled eggs / 1/2 cup seedless grapes / Canadian bacon / cinnamon toast / coffee	frozen yogurt shake / 1/4 cup fresh pineapple / apple bran muffin / coffee	oatmeal with 1/2 banana / faux molasses / rye toast / coffee	sausage fritatta / 1/2 cup blueberries / oat-bran English muffin / coffee
AM snack	V-8 juice / daily vitamin	1/2 cantaloupe / daily vitamin	1/2 cup peaches / daily vitamin	1 medium orange / daily vitamin	1/2 grapefruit / daily vitamin	1/2 cup fresh strawberries / daily vitamin	1 plum / daily vitamin
lunch	minestroni / grilled cheese on multigrain bread / iced coffee latte	1/2 ham & turkey sub on whole grain with Italian dressing & spicy mustard, / 1 cup veggie soup / iced tea	pita fajita: chicken, peppers & onions, / tomato soup / iced tea	pasta fagiole / green salad with Italian dressing & herbed croutons / iced tea	turkey chili / small Caesar's salad with seasoned croutons / iced tea	veggie pocket sandwich / one cup pepper soup / iced tea	1/2 turkey club / cream of potato soup / iced tea
PM snack (optional)	1 oz cheese / small apple	peanut butter and apple jelly sandwich / 1/2 cup low-fat milk	celery sticks with peanut butter / apple juice	fresh squeezed lemonade / herbed popcorn	cinnamon toast / hot mulled cider	5-6 raw carrot sticks / 1 oz peanuts	Hungarian cheese spread with saltine crackers
dinner	salmon patties with horseradish sauce* / steamed broccoli / macaroni & cheese* / corn bread / tea	barbecued chicken / coleslaw / Italian-cut green beans / corn bread / tea	oven-fried catfish / sauteed cabbage & onions / baked beets / herb roll / tea	ham with mustard sauce* / broccoli casserole* / 1/2 baked yam / herb bread sticks / tea	broiled haddock with herbs / steamed asparagus with hollandaise* / wild rice / herb roll / tea	marinated flank steak / cauliflower cheese sauce* / steamed okra / herbed garlic toast / tea	sesame chicken / 1/2 twice-baked potato* / steamed spinach / tea
dessert (optional)	mocha angel food cake / decaf coffee	chocolate cake / decaf coffee	apple spice cake / decaf coffee	banana pudding / decaf coffee	chocolate mousse / decaf coffee	lime Jell-O salad / decaf coffee	sugar cream pie / decaf coffee
before bed snack	cup of hot Ovaltine made with low-fat milk	1/2 cup vanilla yogurt with a pinch of cinnamon	cup of hot Ovaltine made with low-fat milk	1/2 cup apple juice / 1 oz Swiss cheese	1 saltine cracker with peanut butter / 1/2 cup cold low-fat milk	cup of hot Ovaltine made with low-fat milk	1/2 cup vanilla yogurt with a pinch of cinnamon

Remove this page and photocopy at 130% or contact Iron Disorders Institute for enlarged sheet.

Cooking with Less Iron Menu Planner

	day one	day two	day three	day four	day five	day six	day seven
breakfast							
AM snack							
lunch							
PM snack (optional)							
dinner							
dessert (optional)							
before bed snack							

Remove this page and photocopy at 130% or contact Iron Disorders Institute for enlarged sheet.

PHYTATE AND IRON-BINDING POLYPHENOLS *mg/100 g dry matter*

food item	phytate phosphorus	tannin equivalents	chlorogenic acid	TOTAL tannin equivalents
BEVERAGES:				
Coffee		21	71	55
Tea				
English Brkfst		53	14	60
Green		26	17	35
Herb		18		18
Cocoa				
Marabou	504	4400	520	4648
Dutch	513			
Swiss	481			
Beer				
Light lager		0.4		0.4
Whiskey				
Scotch		2.9		2.9
Wine				
White		0	4	2
Red		0.2 to 2.3	20-40	10-21
CEREALS, CRACKERS, BRAN, AND GRAINS:				
Cereals				
Corn flakes	12			
Millet	217			
Oats, rolled	282			
Semolina	19			
Sorghum				
Red	279	480		480
White	389	15		15
Wheat germ	467			
Flours				
Barley	185			
Oat	399-628			
Rice	27			
Wheat	680-1189		58	28
Crackers				
Rye, thin	72-86			
Rye fiber	114-193			
Graham	192			
Oat	166			
Rice cakes	113			

Beverage to Water Ratios:
coffee: 3.3 grams/100mL water or approx. 1oz/3.5 oz
tea: 1 gram /100mL water
Note: 1 milligram of phytate phosphorus= 3.5 milligrams phytic acid

Adapted from chart Hallberg and Hulthén (see bibliography)

food item	phytate phosphorus	tannin equivalents	chlorogenic acid	TOTAL tannin equivalents
CEREALS, CRACKERS, BRAN, AND GRAINS CONTINUED:				
Rice				
Long grain	53-64			
Wild, brown	181-215			
Spaghetti				
Barilla brand	71			
Buitoni brand	6			
FRUITS AND BERRIES:				
Apples	0.1	160		
Apricots				
Avocado	1.0			
Bananas	0.4	40		40
Blackberries	4.0	390		390
Blueberries	6.0	80		80
Currents				
Black	78.0			
Red	55.0			
Dates		5		5
Figs				5
Kiwi	10.0			
Cowberries	5.0	3	250	122
Mangos	1.0			
Melons, honey	0.6			
Oranges	2.0			
Pears	0.2	4	70	37
Raspberries	4.0	70	61	99
Rhubarb	0.2		16	8
Strawberries	4.0			

Note: 1 milligram of phytate phosphorus= 3.5 milligrams phytic acid

Adopted from chart Hallberg and Hulthén (see bibliography)

PHYTATE AND IRON-BINDING POLYPHENOLS *mg/100 g dry matter*				
food item	phytate phosphorus	tannin equivalents	chlorogenic acid	TOTAL tannin equivalents
VEGETABLES:				
Asparagus				
Green	2			
White	3			
Beans				
Black	262			
Brown	195			
Green	15			
Mung	188	140		140
Red	271	1		1
White	269	0		0
Beets	2	3		3
Broccoli	10	1	40	20
Brussel sprouts	11			
Cabbage				
Chinese	2			
White	1			
Carrots	4		28	13
Cauliflower	3			
Celery	5			
Chicory	2			
Corn	24			
Cucumbers	1			
Eggplant	3	7	51	31
Garden cress	7			
Garlic	4		7	3
Horseradish	13			
Leeks	4		11	5
Lentils				
Brown	142	190		190
Red	122			
Lettuce, Iceberg	0.5			
Mushroom	13	1		1
Olives				
Black	3			
Onions				
Red	5	10		10
Yellow	16	6		6

Note: 1 milligram of phytate phosphorus= 3.5 milligrams phytic acid

Adopted from chart Hallberg and Hulthén (see bibliography)

PHYTATE AND IRON-BINDING POLYPHENOLS *mg/100 g dry matter*

food item	phytate phosphorus	tannin equivalents	chlorogenic acid	TOTAL tannin equivalents
SPICES AND HERBS:				
Basil		2.7	7.9	6.5
Caraway		2.8	6.4	5.8
Cardamom		0.3		0.3
Cherval		0.4	2.0	1.4
Cinnamon		43.0	14.3	50.0
Clove		95.0		95.0
Cumin		2.8	6.4	5.8
Curry		6.2	9.9	10.9
Fennel		0.3		0.3
Ginger		0.2		0.2
Marjoram		6.4	9.9	11.1
Oregano	0.2	21.0	6.0	24.0
Pepper				
Black		2.0		2.0
Green		1.4		1.4
Red		0.4		0.8
White		0.4		0.4
Thyme		12.0	4.4	14.1
Turmeric		34.0	0.7	34.0
Vanilla		0.7		0.7
NUTS AND SEEDS:				
Almonds	296.0	43.0		43.0
Brazil nuts		10.0		10.0
Cashews				
Hazelnuts		256.0		256.0
Peanuts				
Walnuts	303.0	1400.0		1400.0
Linseeds	296.0	14.0		14.0
Sesame seeds	576.0			
Sunflower seeds	393	120		120

Note: 1 milligram of phytate phosphorus= 3.5 milligrams phytic acid

Adapted from chart Hallberg and Hulthén (see bibliography)

food item serving size	IRON* MILLIGRAMS		VITAMIN C MILLIGRAMS	FAT GRAMS	CARBOS GRAMS	FIBER GRAMS	PROTEIN GRAMS	CALORIES
	heme	nonheme						
BEVERAGES:								
Beer 8 oz	0.0	-	-	10.8	-	-	1.4	101
Whiskey								
(Scotch) 1 oz	0.0	0.0	-	-	t	-	-	70
Wine 4oz *								
Red dry	0.0	0.5	-	-	1 to 5	-	-	120
White dry	0.0	0.5	-	-	1 to 5	-	-	120
Sweet wines	0.0	0.5	-	-	8 to 9	-	-	120
Soft drinks 12 oz								
Lemon	0.0	0.2	-	-	36.2	-	-	144
Cola	0.0	0.1	-	-	40.0	-	-	154
Ginger ale	0.0	0.7	-	-	33.0	-	-	120
Root beer	0.0	0.2	-	-	42.0	-	-	154
Coffee (1 cup)	0.0	0.1	-	-	0.8	-	-	4
Tea (1 cup)	0.0	0.1	-	-	0.9	-	-	2

*Due to the great variety of wines these numbers represent typical amounts. Consult a more detailed food value composition reference list for specific wines.

food item serving size	IRON* MILLIGRAMS		VITAMIN C MILLIGRAMS	FAT GRAMS	CARBOS GRAMS	FIBER GRAMS	PROTEIN GRAMS	CALORIES
	heme	nonheme						
CONDIMENTS/MISCELLANEOUS:								
Anchovy (3)	0.0	0.93	0.0	1.2	t	-	2.3	21
Bacon bits (¼ oz)	0.0	0.14	0.0	0.3	0.4	-	0.6	7
Barbecue sauce	0.14	0.7	0.3	5.0	-	-	0.2	15
Bouillon (1 cube)								
Beef	0.09	0.08	-	-	1.0	-	-	10
Chicken	0.09	0.08	-	-	1.0	-	-	10
Catsup	0.10	2.5	0.1	4.3	-	-	0.3	19
Garbanzo beans	1.60							
Horseradish			t	-	t	0.5	-	0.1 2
Mustard .	0.10	-	0.8	0.5	-	-	t	11
Olives (1 large)								
Black	0.09	-	0.8	1.0	-	-	-	10
Green	0.09	-	0.8	1.0	-	-	-	10
Pimento	0.00	0.20	t	0.6	0.1	-	0.1	3
Pickle (2 oz)								
Dill	0.0	0.35		t	0.3	0.1	t	1
Sweet	0.0	0.42		-	10.0	-	-	36
Soy sauce	0.0	0.49	-	-	0.9	-	-	10
Vinegar cider	0.0	0.10	-	-	1.0	-	-	2
Worcestershire	0.0	0.30	-	t	t	0.1	-	4

Serving sizes for condiments are one tablespoon unless otherwise specified.
*EXCEPT FOR KNOWN PERCENTAGES: Iron content values for meat are expressed as 40% heme and 60% nonheme.

food item* serving size	IRON MILLIGRAMS heme	IRON MILLIGRAMS nonheme	VITAMIN C MILLIGRAMS	FAT GRAMS	CARBOS GRAMS	FIBER GRAMS	PROTEIN GRAMS	CALORIES
BREADS:								
Biscuit	0.0	0.2	0.0	6.5	17.0		3.0	138
Cinnamon	0.0	0.7	0.0	3.0	15.0	2.0	2.0	90
Cornbread	0.0	1.2	0.0	7.0	29.0	1.7	4.0	200
English muffin	0.0	1.4	0.0	1.0	26.0	2.0	4.0	134
French bread	0.0	0.4	0.0	0.6	11.0		1.8	55
Pita pocket	0.0	1.4	0.0	2.0	33.0		6.0	165
Pumpernickel	0.0	0.8	0.0	4.0	17.0		2.9	79
Raisin	0.0	0.3	0.0	0.6	12.0		1.5	60
Rye	0.0	0.4	0.0	0.3	12.0		2.1	56
Taco shell	0.0	0.3	0.0	2.0	7.0	0.2	1.0	50
Tortilla,Corn	0.0	1.4	0.0	1.0	13.0	0.3	2.0	65
White	0.0	0.7	0.0	1.0	12.0	0.5	2.0	65
Whole wheat	0.0	1.0		1.0	13.0	1.4	3.0	70
CEREALS:								
Bran flakes	0.0	12.4	12.0	1.0	28.0	1.0	4.0	105
Corn flakes	0.0	1.8	15.0		24.0	0.4	2.0	110
Shredded Wheat		1.2		1.0	23.0	3.3	3.0	100
Rice (puffed)	0.0	0.3	0.0	0.1	12.5	0.2	1.0	54
Cream of wheat	0.0	8.2			22.0	0.6	3.0	105
Oatmeal	0.0	1.6		2.0	25.0	4.0	6.0	145
Cornmeal	0.0	4.2	0.0	2.0	43.0	6.8	4.0	210
Cornstarch 1tab	0.0	t		0.0	7.0		0.0	30
CRACKERS:								
Graham	0.0	0.4		1.0	11.0	2.8	1.0	60
Melba	0.0	0.1			4.0		1.0	20
Rye								
Saltine	0.0	0.5		1.0	9.0	0.5	1.0	50
FLOUR:								
Barley	0.0	6.6	0.0	4.0	135.0	32.0	23.0	651
Buckwheat	0.0	4.8	0.0	1.0	41.0	7.1	7.0	190
Oat	0.0	1.6	0.0	2.0	25.0	4.0	6.0	145
Rice	0.0	1.0	0.0	2.0	46.0	4.0	5.0	218
Rye	0.0	2.9	0.0	1.9	79.0		13.0	385
Wheat	0.0	4.6	0.0	2.2	87.1	15.1	16.4	407
Soy	0.0	5.7	0.0	2.4	33.4	3.7	40.9	287
PASTA AND SNACK FOODS								
Macaroni	0.0	2.1	0.0	1.0	39.0	1.2	7.0	190
Popcorn	0.0	0.3		3.0	6.0		1.0	55
Pretzels (per oz.)	0.0	0.3		1.0	13.0		2.0	65
RICE:								
Brown	0.0	0.5	0.0	1.0	25.0	2.4	2.0	115
White	0.0	0.9	0.0		25.0	0.1	2.0	110
Wild	0.0	1.0	0.0	0.6	35.0	0.5	6.5	166

Serving size for bread is one slice. All other portions are one cup unless otherwise specified.

*EXCEPT FOR KNOWN PERCENTAGES: Iron content values for meat are expressed as 40% heme and 60% nonheme.

food item serving size	IRON* MILLIGRAMS		VITAMIN C MILLIGRAMS	FAT GRAMS	CARBOS GRAMS	FIBER GRAMS	PROTEIN GRAMS	CALORIES
	heme	nonheme						
DAIRY:								
Cheese								
American	0.0	0.1	0.0	9.0	0.0	0.0	6.0	105
Bleu	0.0	0.2	0.0	9.0	1.0	0.0	6.0	103
Brie	0.0	0.1	0.0	7.0	0.0	0.0	6.0	85
Cheddar	0.0	0.2	0.0	9.0	0.0	0.0	7.0	113
Cottage								
1 cup	0.0	0.3	0.0	1.0	3.0	0.0	25.0	123
Cream								
1 tblsp.	0.0	0.2	0.0	5.0	0.0	0.0	1.0	51
Feta	0.0	0.1	0.0	6.0	1.1	0.0	4.0	75
Fontina	0.0	t	0.0	8.8	0.4	0.0	7.6	110
Gouda	0.0	t	0.0	7.8	0.6	0.0	8.5	101
Gruyere	0.0	0.3	0.0	8.9	0.5	0.0	8.1	115
Havarti								
Monterey								
jack	0.0	0.2	0.0	8.5	0.2	0.0	6.9	106
Mozzarella	0.0	t	0.0	4.5	0.7	0.0	6.9	72
Muenster	0.0	t	0.0			0.3	6.6	104
Neufchatel	0.0	t	0.0	6.6	0.8	0.0	2.8	74
Parmesan	0.0	0.1	0.0	7.3	0.8	0.0	10.0	110
Provolone	0.0	0.1	0.0	7.5	0.6	0.0	7.3	100
Ricotta (1 cup)	0.0	1.0	0.0	19.4	12.6	0.0	28.0	340
Swiss	0.0	0.2	0.0	7.9	0.5	0.0	7.8	99
Velveeta								
Cream (1 cup)								
Light	0.0	0.0	0.0	28.0	11.1	0.0	7.7	240
Heavy	0.0	0.0	0.0	90.0	7.4	0.0	5.2	861
Sour	0.0	0.0	0.0	43.2	8.0	0.0	6.4	456
Egg (1 lg)								
Yolk only	0.0	0.9	0.0	5.6	t	0.0	2.8	63
White only	0.0	0.1	0.0	0.0	0.4	0.0	3.3	16
Substitute								
1 oz	0.0	0.6	0.0	3.1	0.9	0.0	3.2	45
Ice cream (½ cup)								
plain	0.0	0.6	0.0	7.9	15.9	0.0	2.4	134
Ice milk	0.0	0.9	0.0	4.0	18.0	0.0	3.0	120
Frozen yogurt	0.0	0.1	0.0	1.0	23.0	0.0	3.0	120

Serving size is one ounce unless otherwise specified.
*EXCEPT FOR KNOWN PERCENTAGES: Iron content values for meat are expressed as 40% heme and 60% nonheme.

per serving FOOD VALUES

food item serving size	IRON* MILLIGRAMS		VITAMIN C MILLIGRAMS	FAT GRAMS	CARBOS GRAMS	FIBER GRAMS	PROTEIN GRAMS	CALORIES
	heme	nonheme						
DAIRY CONTINUED:								
Milk (1cup)								
Chocolate	0.0	0.6	0.0	8.5	25.9	0.2	7.9	208
Whole	0.0	0.1	0.0	8.2	11.4	0.0	8.0	150
2%	0.0	0.1	0.0	4.7	11.7	0.0	8.1	121
1%								
Skim	0.0	0.1	0.0	0.1	11.8	0.0	8.4	86
Buttermilk	0.0	0.1	0.0	2.2	11.7	0.0	8.1	99
Canned								
sweetened	0.0	0.5	0.0	26.6	166.5	0.0	24.2	982
condensed	0.0	0.6	0.0	19.1	25.3	0.0	17.2	338
Soy	0.0	1.3	0.0	4.6	4.3	2.6	7.0	79
Yogurt/low-fat								
Vanilla	0.0	t	t	2.8	31.3	0.0	11.2	194
FATS (ONE TABLESPOON):								
Butter		t	0.0	11.5			0.1	101
Margarine		0.0	0.0	11.4				101
Mayonnaise		0.1	0.0	11.0	0.4		0.2	99
Oils								
Canola			0.0	14.0				124
Corn			0.0	13.6				115
Olive			0.0	13.5				120
SALAD DRESSINGS:								
Bleu cheese			0.0	7.7	1.1		0.7	77
French		0.1	0.0	6.1	2.7	0.1	0.1	67
Italian			0.0	6.8	1.5		0.1	68
Ranch		0.1	0.0	5.0	1.0		0.0	50
Thousand Island		0.1	0.0	5.3	2.4	0.3	0.1	59

Serving size is one ounce unless otherwise specified.
*EXCEPT FOR KNOWN PERCENTAGES: Iron content values for meat are expressed as 40% heme and 60% nonheme.

food item	serving size	IRON* MILLIGRAMS		VITAMIN C MILLIGRAMS	FAT GRAMS	CARBOS GRAMS	FIBER GRAMS	PROTEIN GRAMS	CALORIES
		heme	nonheme						
FRUITS:									
Apples		0.0	0.25	8	0.5	21.0	1.0	0.2	81
Applesauce		0.0	0.29	2	0.1	27.5	1.3	0.4	106
Apricots		0.0							
Fresh		0.0	0.58	11	0.4	11.7	0.6	1.4	51
Dried (10 halves)		0.0	1.65	1	0.1	21.6	1.0	1.2	83
Avocados		0.0	2.05	24	30.8	14.8	4.2	4.0	324
Bananas		0.0	0.35	10	0.5	26.7	0.5	1.2	105
Blackberries		0.0	0.24	15	0.5	20.5	1.8	0.9	82
Blueberries		0.0	1.12	9	0.3	16.0	3.5	1.4	66
Cherries		0.0	0.56	5	1.4	24.0	0.6	1.7	104
Cranberries		0.0	0.19	13	0.2	12.0	1.1	0.3	46
Dates (10)		0.0	0.96	-	0.3	61.0	1.8	1.6	228
Grapefruit (½)		0.0	0.10	41	0.1	9.7	0.2	0.7	38
Grapes		0.0	0.30	5	0.3	15.7	0.7	0.5	58
Kiwi (1)		0.0	0.30	74	0.3	11.3	0.8	0.7	46
Limes (1 oz)		0.0	0.01	9	-	2.8	-	0.1	8
Mango		0.0	0.20	57	0.5	35.0	1.7	1.0	135
Melon (½)		0.0	0.50	58	0.7	22.0	0.9	2.3	94
Oranges		0.0	0.6	96	0.1	15.4	0.5	1.2	62
Peaches		0.0	0.1	12	-	9.6	0.5	0.6	37
Pears		0.0	0.2	7	0.6	25.0	2.3	0.6	98
Pineapples		0.0	0.6	24	0.6	19.2	0.8	0.6	77
Plums		0.0	0.1	12	0.4	8.6	0.4	0.5	36
Prunes (10)		0.0	2.0	4	-	52.7	1.7	2.1	201
Raisins		0.0	4.3	4	0.9	12.9	1.1	4.2	488
Raspberries		0.0	0.7	50	0.7	14.2	3.7	1.1	61
Strawberries		0.0	0.5	85	0.5	10.4	0.8	0.9	45
Watermelon		0.0	0.3	15	0.6	11.5	0.48	1.0	50

per serving FOOD VALUES

Serving size is one cup unless otherwise specified.
*EXCEPT FOR KNOWN PERCENTAGES: Iron content values for meat are expressed as 40% heme and 60% nonheme.

food item serving size	IRON* MILLIGRAMS		VITAMIN C MILLIGRAMS	per serving FOOD VALUES FAT GRAMS	CARBOS GRAMS	FIBER GRAMS	PROTEIN GRAMS	CALORIES
	heme	nonheme						
BEEF:								
Brisket	0.55	1.6	0.0	14.2	0.1	0.0	21.8	222
Chuck roast	1.18	1.2	0.0	22.5	0.0	0.0	20.7	291
Dried beef (1oz)	0.64	0.6	0.0	1.1	4.4	0.0	8.2	47
Flank steak	0.55	1.6	0.0	14.2	0.1	0.0	21.8	222
Ground (lean)	0.8	1.2	0.0	9.7	0.0	0.0	5.0	224
Liver	3.0	4.6	0.0	4.3	6.5	0.0	22.6	161
Prime rib	0.95	0.9	0.0	33.0	0.0	0.0	18.2	375
Round steak	1.05	1.0	0.0	19.8	0.0	0.0	22.0	273
Sirloin	1.25	1.2	0.0	22.8	0.0	0.0	20.6	294
Tenderloin	1.35	1.3	0.0	20.4	0.0	0.0	21.0	275
POULTRY:								
Chicken (3.2 oz)								
Breast	0.4	0.7	0.0	4.2	0.0	0.0	27.0	154
Dark meat	0.5	0.8	0.0	10.0	0.0	0.0	27.0	203
Turkey								
Breast	0.4	0.7	0.0	3.5	0.0	0.0	29.8	91
Dark meat	0.5	0.8	0.0	4.0	0.0	0.0	16.0	104
PORK:								
Bacon (1 strip)	0.15	0.5	0.0	14.7	0.0	0.0	2.4	157
Canadian bacon	0.18	0.6	0.0	19.8	0.0	0.0	23.4	178
Ham	0.25	0.8	0.0	25.0	0.0	0.0	19.9	206
Pork chop (5oz)	0.18	0.6	0.0	43.0	0.0	0.0	20.0	345
Shoulder	0.25	0.8	0.0	25.7	0.0	0.0	18.2	312
Tenderloin	0.2	0.7	0.0	5.0	0.0	0.0	17.0	186
Roast	0.18	0.6	0.0	34.2	0.0	0.0	25.5	422
Spareribs	0.15	0.5	0.0	33.0	0.0	0.0	12.0	201
VENISON (3.2 oz.):	2.3	2.2	0.0	3.6	0.0	0.0	19.0	114
VEAL (3 oz):								
Breast	0.3	0.5	0.0	5.0	0.0	0.0	22.0	143
Roast	0.3	0.5	0.0	8.0	0.0	0.0	29.0	192

Serving size is 3 ounces unless otherwise specified.

*EXCEPT FOR KNOWN PERCENTAGES: Iron content values for meat are expressed as 40% heme and 60% nonheme.

food item serving size	IRON* MILLIGRAMS		VITAMIN C MILLIGRAMS	per serving FOOD VALUES				
				FAT GRAMS	CARBOS GRAMS	FIBER GRAMS	PROTEIN GRAMS	CALORIES
	heme	nonheme						
LUNCHEON MEAT:								
Beef bologna	0.1	0.2	–	9.1	0.4	0.5	3.3	89
Pork bologna	t	0.1	–	9.1	0.6	0.2	4.3	70
Italian sausage	0.4	0.6	–	8.9	0.2	0.0	4.0	98
Pepperoni	t	t	–	13.0	0.0	0.0	6.0	140
Polish sausage	0.1	0.2	–	8.1	0.5	0.0	4.0	92
Pork sausage	t	0.1	–	8.8	0.3	0.0	5.6	105
Pork salami	t	t	–	9.6	0.2	0.0	6.4	115
Turkey hot dog	t	0.1	–	5.0	0.4	0.0	4.1	64
MISCELLANEOUS:								

Serving size is one ounce unless otherwise specified.
*EXCEPT FOR KNOWN PERCENTAGES: Iron content values for meat are expressed as 40% heme and 60% nonheme.

food item serving size	IRON* MILLIGRAMS		VITAMIN C MILLIGRAMS	FAT GRAMS	CARBOS GRAMS	FIBER GRAMS	PROTEIN GRAMS	CALORIES
	heme	nonheme						
NUTS AND SEEDS:								
Almonds	0.0	6.7	0.0	77	27.7	3.8	26.4	849
Cashews	0.0	5.3	0.0	64	41.0	1.9	24.1	785
Coconut	0.0	1.4	0.0	28.2	7.5	2.7	2.8	277
Hazelnuts	0.0	4.6	0.0	84.2	22.5	1.1	17.0	856
Macadamia nuts	0.0	3.2	0.0	98.8	18.4	7.1	11.0	940
Peanuts	0.0	3.2	0.0	70.1	29.7	3.9	37.7	838
Pecans	0.0	2.6	0.0	76.9	15.8	2.3	9.9	742
Pistachios	0.0	8.6	0.0	61.9	31.7	2.4	26.0	739
Pumpkin seeds	0.0	15.7	0.0	65.4	21.0	2.7	40.6	774
Sesame seeds	0.0	3.6	0.0	80	26.4	3.6	27.3	873
Sunflower seeds	0.0	10.3	0.0	68.6	28.9	5.5	34.8	812
Walnuts	0.0	3.1	0.0	64	15.8	2.1	14.8	651
Peanut butter	0.0	0.3	0.0	8.1	3.2	0.3	3.9	86

per serving **FOOD VALUES**

MISCELLANEOUS:

Serving size is one ounce unless otherwise specified.

*EXCEPT FOR KNOWN PERCENTAGES: Iron content values for meat are expressed as 40% heme and 60% nonheme.

food item serving size	IRON*		VITAMIN C	FAT	FOOD VALUES			
	MILLIGRAMS		MILLIGRAMS	GRAMS	CARBOS GRAMS	FIBER GRAMS	PROTEIN GRAMS	CALORIES
	heme	nonheme						
SEAFOOD:								
Anchovies (5)	0.37	0.5	0	1.9	0.0	0	5.8	42
Catfish	0.4	0.6	0	3.6	0.0	0	15.5	99
Caviar (1T)	0.7	1.0	0	2.8	0.6	0	3.9	40
Clams (9)	10.0	15.0	0	0.6	4.6	0	23.0	130
Cod	t	0.1	0	0.6	0.0	0	15.0	70
Crab	0.2	0.3	0	0.5	0.0	0	15.6	71
Haddock	0.4	0.6	0	0.6	0.0	0	16.0	70
Halibut	0.3	0.4	0	2.0	0.0	0	17.7	93
Herring	0.4	0.5	0	7.7	0.0	0	15.0	134
Lobster	0.2	0.3	0	0.7	0.4	0	16.0	77
Mackerel	0.5	0.8	0	2.8	0.0	0	22.8	114
Oysters (6)	2.2	3.3	0	2.1	0.0	0	5.9	58
Perch	0.3	0.5	0	1.4	0.0	0	15.8	80
Pollack	0.2	0.2	0	0.8	0.0	0	16.4	75
Salmon	0.3	0.4	0	6.0	0.0	0	17.0	121
Sardines (2)	0.3	0.4	0	2.7	0.0	0	5.9	50
Scallops	t	0.1	0	0.6	0.0	0	14.3	75
Shrimp	0.8	1.2	0	1.5	0.0	0	17.3	90
Snails (escargot)	1.7	2.6	0	0.3	0.0	0	6.6	20
Snapper	t	t	0	1.0	0.0	0	17.4	85
Swordfish	0.3	0.4	0	3.4	0.0	0	16.8	103
Trout	0.5	0.8	0	5.6	0.0	0	17.7	126
Tuna	1.1	1.7	0	0.6	0.0	0	20.0	94
Whitefish	0.1	0.1	0	5.0	0.0	0	16.0	114

Serving size is 3 ounces unless otherwise specified.
*EXCEPT FOR KNOWN PERCENTAGES: Iron content values for meat are expressed as 40% heme and 60% nonheme.

food item serving size	IRON* MILLIGRAMS		VITAMIN C MILLIGRAMS	FAT GRAMS	FOOD VALUES			
	heme	nonheme			CARBOS GRAMS	FIBER GRAMS	PROTEIN GRAMS	CALORIES
VEGETABLES:								
Artichoke	0.0	1.1	8.0	0.2	9.9	6.0	2.8	44
Asparagus								
(1 spear)	0.0	0.1	5.3	0.6	0.6	-	0.3	16
Beans								
Black	0.0	5.2	0.0	1.0	40.8	7.2	15.2	226
Green	0.0	0.7	0.2	8.9	10.0	4.0	2.0	44
Kidney	0.0	5.2	2.0	1.0	40.0	13.0	15.0	225
Lima	0.0	4.4	0.0	1.0	42.0	14.0	15.0	229
Navy	0.0	2.5	0.0	0.0	19.0	4.0	7.0	109
Pinto	0.0	2.2	2.0	0.4	43.6	6.8	14.0	234
Beets	0.0	0.5	5.0	t	5.7	0.7	0.9	26
Broccoli	0.0	0.6	58.0	0.2	3.9	2.0	2.3	22
Brussels								
sprouts	0.0	0.5	0.5	0.4	6.8	3.4	2.0	30
Cabbage	0.0	0.2	18.0	0.1	1.9	0.4	0.4	8
Carrots	0.0	0.2	2.0	0.1	5.6	1.8	0.6	24
Cauliflower	0.0	0.2	36.0	0.1	2.9	1.4	1.2	15
Celery	0.0	0.2	4.0	0.1	2.2	1.0	0.5	10
Collards	0.0	0.1	8.0	t	1.3	0.1	0.3	6
Corn	0.0	0.5	5.0	1.1	20.6	3.0	2.7	89
Cucumber	0.0	0.1	2.0	0.1	1.5	0.5	0.3	7
Eggplant	0.0	0.2	1.0	0.1	3.2	0.5	0.4	13
Garlic (1 clove)	0.0	t	1.0	t	1.0	0.1	0.2	4
Kale	0.0	0.6	27.0	0.3	3.7	0.5	1.2	21
Kohlrabi	0.0	0.3	44.0	0.1	5.5	0.9	1.5	24
Leeks	0.0	0.6	2.0	0.2	7.4	0.6	0.8	32
Lettuce								
Bibb	0.0	0.5	13.0	0.1	0.7	0.3	0.4	4
Iceberg	0.0	0.3	1.0	0.1	0.6	0.3	0.3	4
Leaf	0.0	0.4	5.0	0.1	1.0	0.2	0.4	5
Romaine	0.0	0.3	7.0	0.1	0.7	0.5	0.5	4
Mushrooms	0.0	0.4	1.0	0.2	1.6	0.5	0.7	9
Mustard greens	0.0	0.5	10.0	0.1	1.4	0.2	0.8	7
Okra	0.0	0.4	13.0	0.1	3.8	0.5	1.0	25
Onions	0.0	0.2	5.0	0.1	6.9	1.3	0.9	30
Parsley	0.0	1.8	27.0	0.1	2.1	1.3	0.7	10
Parsnips	0.0	0.4	10.0	0.2	15.2	2.1	1.0	63
Peas	0.0	1.2	11.0	0.2	12.5	3.0	4.3	67
Peppers								
Green	0.0	0.2	45.0	0.1	3.2	0.8	0.4	13
Red	0.0	0.2	95.0	0.1	3.2	0.8	0.4	13

Serving size is one half cup unless otherwise specified.

*EXCEPT FOR KNOWN PERCENTAGES: Iron content values for meat are expressed as 40% heme and 60% nonheme.

food item serving size	IRON* MILLIGRAMS		VITAMIN C MILLIGRAMS	FAT GRAMS	per serving FOOD VALUES CARBOS GRAMS	FIBER GRAMS	PROTEIN GRAMS	CALORIES
	heme	nonheme						
VEGETABLES CONTINUED:								
Peppers								
Green	0.0	0.2	45.0	0.1	3.2	0.8	0.4	13
Red	0.0	0.2	95.0	0.1	3.2	0.8	0.4	13
Potatoes								
Sweet	0.0	0.7	25.0	0.1	24.3	3.0	1.7	103
White	0.0	0.8	26.0	0.1	24.4	1.0	2.2	105
w/skin	0.0	2.7	15.0	0.2	51.0	5.3	4.7	220
Pumpkin	0.0	0.7	6.0	0.1	6.0	1.0	0.9	24
Radishes (10)	0.0	0.1	10.0	0.2	1.6	0.2	0.3	7
Sauerkraut	0.0	1.7	17.0	0.2	5.1	1.3	1.0	22
Spinach	0.0	0.7	8.0	0.1	1.0	0.7	0.8	6
Squash	0.0	0.6	8.0	t	8.0	3.0	1.0	29
Tomatoes	0.0	0.4	17.0	0.3	4.2	1.2	0.8	19
Zucchini	0.0	0.3	4.0	0.1	1.9	0.3	0.8	9
MISCELLANEOUS:								

Serving size is one cup unless otherwise specified.
*EXCEPT FOR KNOWN PERCENTAGES: Iron content values for meat are expressed as 40% heme and 60% nonheme.

food item serving size	IRON* MILLIGRAMS heme	nonheme	VITAMIN C MILLIGRAMS	FAT GRAMS	CARBOS GRAMS	FIBER GRAMS	PROTEIN GRAMS	CALORIES	BETA-CAROTENE Mcg/100 GRAMS EDIBLE PORTION

per serving **FOOD VALUES**

Calculate iron content of meat at 40% heme and 60% nonheme unless otherwise specified.

SHOPPING LIST

USE A HIGHLIGHTER TO NOTE WHICH FOODS YOU WISH TO PURCHASE

PRODUCE:
Lettuce
  Romaine
  Iceberg
  Bibb
  Other
Cabbage
  Green
  Savoy
  Red
Onions
  Yellow
  White
  Vidalia
  Spring
Spinach
Chives
Parsley
Tomatoes
Cucumbers
Radishes
Asparagus
Beans
Cauliflower
Broccoli
Squash
Peas
Potatoes
  Red
  Sweet
  Idaho/russet

FRUIT:
Apples
Grapes
Cherries
Peaches
Pears
Strawberries
Blueberries
Raspberries
Blackberries
Pineapple
Oranges
Watermelon
Melon
Kiwi
Bananas

DAIRY:
Sour cream
Milk
Buttermilk
Heavy cream
Light cream
Butter
Yogurt
Eggs

CHEESES:
Monterey jack
Mozzarella
Parmesan
Swiss
Fontina
Havarti
Cheddar
Other:

MEAT:
Chicken breast
Chicken dark meat
Chicken whole
Chicken/ground
Turkey breast
Turkey breast/ground
Turkey dark meat
Turkey whole
Veal cutlets
Veal/ground
Veal roast
Veal stew meat
Ham steak
Ham picnic shoulder
Pork filet
Pork roast
Pork stew meat
Pork/ground
Beef sirloin/ground
Beef sirloin steak
Beef filet

FISH:
Bass
Flounder
Grouper
Halibut
Mackerel
Perch
Orange roughy
Salmon
Shrimp
Snapper
Sole
Swordfish
Tuna
Trout

FROZEN:
Yogurt
Pie crust
Other:

DRY GOODS:
Flour
Cornmeal
Beans
Rice
Pasta

SPICES/HERBS:
Bay leaf
Basil
Cumin
Greek
Garlic
Marjoram
Oregano
Rosemary
Red pepper
black pepper
White pepper
Sage
Salt
Thyme
Cinnamon
Nutmeg
Ginger

CANNED GOODS:
Tomates diced
Tomato paste
Tomato sauce

OILS/CONDIMENTS:
Apple cider vinegar
Brown sugar
Catsup
Coffee
Olive oil
Olives
Tea

Banana Pineapple Cooler

Serves 1

1	medium banana, not overripe
¼	cup fresh pineapple
½	cup apple juice
1	teaspoon sugar
½	cup pineapple sherbet

In a blender combine all ingredients and blend on high speed.
Serve over ice.

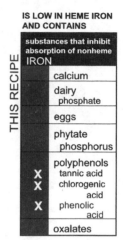

IS LOW IN HEME IRON AND CONTAINS

THIS RECIPE	substances that inhibit absorption of nonheme IRON	
		calcium
		dairy phosphate
		eggs
		phytate phosphorus
	X	polyphenols tannic acid
	X	chlorogenic acid
	X	phenolic acid
		oxalates

IRON	per serving	
	heme iron MILLIGRAMS	nonheme iron MILLIGRAMS
	0.0	0.6

Faux Whiskey Sour

Serves 1

½   cup brewed tea
2   ounces Wild Turkey whiskey
2   tablespoons frozen lemonade

In a small saucepan combine all of the ingredients and bring to a boil. Remove from the heat and place in the freezer to cool.

   Serve over cracked ice.

   Note: Alcohol enhances the absorption of iron and frequent consumption of alcoholic beverages can cause liver disease. Alcohol has a lower boiling point than water and so by bringing the liquid to a boil the alcohol content is burned out without losing the flavor of the whiskey. This recipe contains tannins, chlorogenic acid.

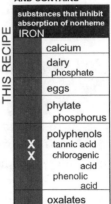

IS LOW IN HEME IRON AND CONTAINS	
substances that inhibit absorption of nonheme IRON	
	calcium
	dairy phosphate
	eggs
	phytate phosphorus
X	polyphenols tannic acid
X	chlorogenic acid
	phenolic acid
	oxalates

THIS RECIPE

per serving		
IRON	heme iron MILLIGRAMS	nonheme iron MILLIGRAMS
	0.0	0.1

Fresh Squeezed Lemonade

Serves 8

¾   cup sugar
¾   cup hot water
1   cup lemon juice (about 12 lemons)
7   cups water

In a pitcher dissolve the sugar in the hot water. Add the lemon juice and water.

   Stir and serve over ice.

   Note: This is a high vitamin C beverage and is a good choice for snacks and to drink when taking a daily multivitamin.

IS LOW IN HEME IRON AND CONTAINS	
substances that inhibit absorption of nonheme IRON	
	calcium
	dairy phosphate
	eggs
	phytate phosphorus
X	polyphenols tannic acid
X	chlorogenic acid
	phenolic acid
	oxalates

THIS RECIPE

per serving		
IRON	heme iron MILLIGRAMS	nonheme iron MILLIGRAMS
	0.0	0.1

Hot Cocoa

Serves 6

6	tablespoons cocoa powder
6	tablespoons sugar
	Dash salt
1	cup water
2	cups milk
1	cup light cream or half and half

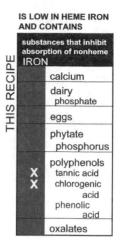

IS LOW IN HEME IRON AND CONTAINS		
substances that inhibit absorption of nonheme IRON		
	calcium	
	dairy phosphate	
	eggs	
	phytate phosphorus	
X X	polyphenols tannic acid chlorogenic acid phenolic acid	
	oxalates	

In a saucepan combine the cocoa, sugar, salt, and water. Bring to a boil, stirring constantly with a wooden spoon until liquid will coat the back of the spoon. Reduce the heat and stir in the milk. Add the cream. Serve with marshmallows or whipped cream topping.

Chocolate contains high levels of tannins and chlorogenic acid; this old-fashioned recipe is a good alternative to a cup of coffee or tea.

IRON	*per serving*	
	heme iron MILLIGRAMS	nonheme iron MILLIGRAMS
	0.0	trace

Mulled Cider

Serves 8

2	quarts apple cider
½	cup brown sugar
1¼	teaspoons ground cinnamon
1¼	teaspoons allspice
1	tablespoon whole cloves

IS LOW IN HEME IRON AND CONTAINS		
substances that inhibit absorption of nonheme IRON		
	calcium	
	dairy phosphate	
	eggs	
	phytate phosphorus	
X X X	polyphenols tannic acid chlorogenic acid phenolic acid	
	oxalates	

In a saucepan simmer the cider on the stovetop. Add the sugar and spices, and bring to a gentle boil. Cover, cut off the heat, and steep for 20 minutes. Do not remove the cover until 20 minutes have lapsed.

IRON	*per serving*	
	heme iron MILLIGRAMS	nonheme iron MILLIGRAMS
	0.0	0.6

Peach Frost

Serves 1

½   **cup sliced fresh peaches**
½   **cup apple juice**
1   **cup frozen vanilla yogurt**

In a blender combine all of the ingredients and blend well. Serve in a tall chilled glass.

IRON	per serving heme iron MILLIGRAMS	nonheme iron MILLIGRAMS
	0.0	0.1

IS LOW IN HEME IRON AND CONTAINS

THIS RECIPE	substances that inhibit absorption of nonheme IRON	
		calcium
	X	dairy phosphate
		eggs
		phytate phosphorus
	X X	polyphenols tannic acid chlorogenic acid phenolic acid
		oxalates

Raspberry Faux Champagne

Serves 4

2   **cups chilled white grape juice**
2   **cups chilled ginger ale**
4   **tablespoons frozen raspberries with syrup**

In a pitcher mix all of the ingredients together. Serve in fluted glasses.

IRON	per serving heme iron MILLIGRAMS	nonheme iron MILLIGRAMS
	0.0	0.3

IS LOW IN HEME IRON AND CONTAINS

THIS RECIPE	substances that inhibit absorption of nonheme IRON	
		calcium
		dairy phosphate
		eggs
		phytate phosphorus
	X X X	polyphenols tannic acid chlorogenic acid phenolic acid
		oxalates

Spiced Chocolate Shake
Serves 4

1 ½	**cups milk**
2	**tablespoons instant coffee**
½	**teaspoon ground cinnamon**
¼	**teaspoon ground cloves**
2	**cups chocolate ice cream**
	Chocolate shavings

In a blender combine all ingredients. Blend until combined. Serve in chilled glasses with chocolate shavings as garnish.

THIS RECIPE	IS LOW IN HEME IRON AND CONTAINS	
	substances that inhibit absorption of nonheme IRON	
		calcium
	X	dairy phosphate
		eggs
		phytate phosphorus
	X	polyphenols tannic acid
	X	chlorogenic acid
		phenolic acid
		oxalates

IRON	per serving heme iron MILLIGRAMS	nonheme iron MILLIGRAMS
	0.0	0.4

Coffee

Coffee was first cultivated in Arabia more than five hundred years ago. During the sixteenth and seventeenth centuries, coffee from the islands of Mocha and Java was introduced all over Europe, where coffeehouses became commonplace. American coffeehouses were first established as early as 1689 in Boston, New York, and Philadelphia.

Most coffees are derived from two species of beans: arabica and robusta. Arabicas offer the finest aroma and flavor, are less acidic, and have less caffeine than robustas coffees. American coffees are of the robusta beans. Coffees are labeled by either the darkness of the roast or by the region where the bean was grown. The majority of coffee is grown in Africa, Central and South America, and Indonesia. It is also grown in Hawaii, the Caribbean, New Guinea, India, and the Middle East.

Coffee beans are picked green and roasted, which provides the rich flavor.

Roasting typically takes from 1 to 17 minutes at temperatures between 380° and 480°F. The longer the roast, the deeper the flavor and color of the beans. The degree of roast is designated by names such as American and French Roast. Roast time and temperature also depend on moisture content and density of the beans.

Tannin or tannic acid contained in coffee can inhibit the absorption of nutrients, especially minerals such as iron. Tannin makes up about 8 percent of a green coffee bean and is what gives coffee its bite.

Coffee can also stimulate the production of stomach acid, which probably accounts for the reason why tea is a better inhibitor of iron absorption than coffee. Studies demonstrate that one cup of strong coffee drank within two hours of meal consumption impaired absorption of iron up to 60 percent, while tea can inhibit iron absorption by as much as 80 to 90 percent.

How to brew coffee:

There are three basic brewing methods: drip, vacuum, and percolator, but all methods require 1 tablespoon of coffee to 8 ounces of water, unless stronger coffee is preferred.

Drip coffee method: Water is poured into a reservoir where it is heated and flows over coffee contained in a basket. Brewed coffee drips into a glass pot.

Vacuum coffee method: Hot water is placed in the upper portion of a two-part glass or metal coffee maker. The hot water is pressed over the coffee and forced into the bottom portion of the maker.

Percolator method: Coffeemakers are usually electric. Water is placed in the coffeemaker and a basket containing coffee is held by a stem that is inserted into the pot. The boiling water percolates up through the stem, pouring onto the coffee and seeping out into the water below.

Espresso is a method of brewing more than a type of coffee. Although one can purchase coffee labeled espresso, the term comes from the Italian word meaning "fast."

Espresso was invented in 1903 by Luigi Bezzera, the owner of a manufacturing business. He was not happy because his employees were taking too long for their coffee breaks. In an effort to shorten breaks and increase productivity Bezzera found a way to shorten the brewing process used to make traditional coffee. He invented a machine that used pressure in the brewing process, reducing the time needed to brew a pot of coffee. He called his new machine the "Fast Coffee Machine", which would make a cup of coffee in just 20 seconds.

Café Vienna

Serves 4

4	cups strong hot coffee plus 1 tablespoon instant coffee
½	cup heavy cream
¼	cup Faux Molasses, or to taste (see recipe on page 216)
½	teaspoon ground cinnamon

Pour the coffee into a clean tea pot or coffee carafe. Dissolve the instant coffee in the hot coffee.

Add cream, syrup, and cinnamon.

Garnish each serving with a dollop of whipped cream and a sprinkle of cinnamon, and serve promptly.

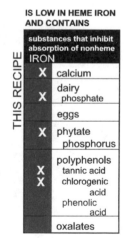

	IS LOW IN HEME IRON AND CONTAINS
	substances that inhibit absorption of nonheme IRON
X	calcium
X	dairy phosphate
	eggs
X	phytate phosphorus
X X	polyphenols tannic acid chlorogenic acid phenolic acid
	oxalates

THIS RECIPE

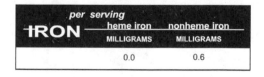

IRON	per serving		
	heme iron MILLIGRAMS	nonheme iron MILLIGRAMS	
	0.0	0.7	

Iced Coffee

Serves 4

4	cups brewed coffee
2	tablespoons instant coffee
3	tablespoons Faux Molasses (see recipe on page 216)
½	cup milk

In a pitcher combine the coffee, molasses, and milk. Pour over ice. Serve with a straw.

	IS LOW IN HEME IRON AND CONTAINS
	substances that inhibit absorption of nonheme IRON
X	calcium
X	dairy phosphate
	eggs
X	phytate phosphorus
X X	polyphenols tannic acid chlorogenic acid phenolic acid
	oxalates

THIS RECIPE

IRON	per serving		
	heme iron MILLIGRAMS	nonheme iron MILLIGRAMS	
	0.0	0.6	

Mocha Café Latte Hot

Serves 4

2   cups strong coffee
2   cups scalded milk
4   tablespoons Nestle's brand instant cocoa

In a saucepan combine the coffee, milk, and cocoa. Mix well. Serve in warm mugs.

Mocha Café Latte Chilled

2   cups strong coffee
2   tablespoons instant coffee
2   cups scalded milk
6   tablespoons Nestle's brand instant cocoa

In a saucepan combine the brewed coffee, instant coffee, milk, and cocoa. Cool and serve over ice.

THIS RECIPE	IS LOW IN HEME IRON AND CONTAINS	
	substances that inhibit absorption of nonheme IRON	
	X	calcium
	X	dairy phosphate
		eggs
	X	phytate phosphorus
	X X	polyphenols tannic acid chlorogenic acid phenolic acid
		oxalates

IRON	per serving	
	heme iron MILLIGRAMS	nonheme iron MILLIGRAMS
	0.0	0.7

Tea

According to Chinese legend, tea has been around for more than five thousand years. During this ancient period, the emperor ruled that all drinking water was to be boiled as a hygienic precaution. One summer day while traveling, servants to the emperor were preparing a pot of boiling water. Dried tea leaves accidentally landed in the pot. Curious about the taste, the emperor drank the concoction and reported that he felt good afterward. And so, according to legend, tea was created.

From China, tea was introduced to Japan by a returning Buddhist priest and to Europe by a Portuguese Jesuit missionary. Tea was transported by the Portuguese to Lisbon and Dutch ships transported it to France, Holland, and the Baltic countries.

In the 1600s tea became popular throughout Europe, Russia, and the American colonies. Russian interest in tea began as early as 1618. Dutch explorer Peter Stuyvesant brought the first tea to America in 1650 to the colonists in the Dutch settlement of New Amsterdam (later renamed New York by the English). The first samples of tea reached England between 1652 and 1654. Tea quickly proved popular enough to replace ale as the national drink of England.

Today American schoolchildren learn about the famous Boston Tea Party where our colonial forefathers protested the British tea tax, an act that eventually led to the start of the Revolutionary War. During this century, two major American contributions to the tea industry occurred. In 1904, iced tea was created at the World's Fair in St. Louis, and in 1908, Thomas Sullivan of New York developed the concept of tea in a bag.

All tea comes from an evergreen shrub called the *Camellia sinensis* plant. Even though there are more than 1,500 different blends of tea, all blends are derived from just three types of tea: black, green and oolong. The difference comes in how the tea leaves are processed. Tea leaves are picked and rolled then allowed to wither and then to ferment or oxidize. The dark substances that form while the tea leaves are exposed to the air are produced by the chemical reactions of the tannins in the tea. They give the tea astringency, robust flavor, and aroma, and they leach into hot water to produce the characteristic reddish amber color. The oxidizing stage of tea processing does not take long, no more than four hours. When the leaves have transformed sufficiently, then they are "fired," dried over heat to stop the oxidation process. The length of time leaves oxidize determines the type of tea.

Black tea ferments the longest; well-known types of black tea include: orange pekoe, Darjeeling, Earl Grey, and English breakfast.

Green tea skips the oxidizing step. Instead, the leaves are steamed right after the withering stage, which destroys the enzymes that would otherwise cause the darkening. The steamed leaves are rolled and immediately fired.

Because the tannins do not go through the oxidizing process, which has a mellowing effect, green tea can be bitter and more astringent than black, especially if it is steeped for a long time.

Oolongs are "semi-fermented" teas. That is, they are processed the same way black teas are, but they aren't allowed to oxidize fully.

Herbal teas are not true teas. They are infusions or *tisane* (tee-zonh), which is French for "herbal drink." Popular infusions include rose hips, peppermint, and chamomile. Some herbal "teas" provide health benefits and some, such as peppermint, contain substances (possibly oxalates) that inhibit the absorption of nonheme iron.

Health benefits of drinking tea
Scientists continue to report findings that iron excesses can contribute to heart disease and nourish cancer cells and that drinking tea reduces the risk of these chronic illnesses. Teas contain tannins and chlorogenic acid, two polyphenols that inhibit the absorption of nonheme iron. Polyphenols are powerful antioxidants, which combat free radical activity.

How to brew tea
In a saucepan bring fresh cold water to a full rolling boil. Measure 1 teaspoon of tea or 1 tea bag per cup of water. Cut off the heat and drop the tea bags into the water. Allow tea to steep 3 to 5 minutes, depending on the strength you like.

Note: If using loose tea, cheesecloth or a tea infuser can hold the tea while it steeps, or hot water can be poured directly over the tea leaves and strained after steeping. Remove the tea bags and add sugar if desired. Do not add sugar to boiling water, this can cause an injury.

Cranberry Cherry Tea

Serves 8 to 10

8	**cups brewed tea**
½	**cup grenadine**
1	**cup cranberry juice**

In a pitcher combine all of the ingredients. Serve over ice.

THIS RECIPE	IS LOW IN HEME IRON AND CONTAINS	
	substances that inhibit absorption of nonheme	
	IRON	
		calcium
		dairy phosphate
		eggs
		phytate phosphorus
	X	polyphenols tannic acid
	X	chlorogenic acid
		phenolic acid
	X	oxalates

IRON	per serving	
	heme iron MILLIGRAMS	nonheme iron MILLIGRAMS
	0.0	0.6

Lemon Tea

Serves 8 to 10

¾	**cup sugar**
¾	**cup hot water**
1	**cup lemon juice (about 12 lemons)**
7	**cups brewed tea**

In a saucepan dissolve the sugar in the hot water. Set aside.

In a separate pan boil water to brew the tea. As the water boils, add the lemon juice. Allow the lemon water to boil rapidly for 20 to 30 seconds before adding the tea bags. Cut off the heat; allow the tea to steep. When fully steeped, stir in the sugar water and serve over ice .

THIS RECIPE	IS LOW IN HEME IRON AND CONTAINS	
	substances that inhibit absorption of nonheme	
	IRON	
		calcium
		dairy phosphate
		eggs
		phytate phosphorus
	X	polyphenols tannic acid
	X	chlorogenic acid
		phenolic acid
		oxalates

IRON	per serving	
	heme iron MILLIGRAMS	nonheme iron MILLIGRAMS
	0.0	0.4

Lime Zinger
Serves 8

2	tablespoons sugar
7	cups brewed green tea
¾	cup lime juice
3	cups ginger ale

In a pitcher dissolve the sugar in the warm tea. Add the lime juice and ginger ale.

Serve over ice.

IS LOW IN HEME IRON AND CONTAINS	
substances that inhibit absorption of nonheme	
IRON	
	calcium
	dairy phosphate
	eggs
	phytate phosphorus
X	polyphenols tannic acid
X	chlorogenic acid
	phenolic acid
	oxalates

(THIS RECIPE)

IRON	per serving	
	heme iron MILLIGRAMS	nonheme iron MILLIGRAMS
	0.0	0.7

Spiced Tea Hot or Chilled
Serves 8

4	cups water
1	family-sized Lipton brand tea bag
½	teaspoon each: cinnamon, cloves, ginger
4	tablespoons sugar
2	cups apple cider
	Cinnamon sticks

In a saucepan bring the water to a boil. Pour over the tea bag and spices, and steep for 4 to 5 minutes. Add the sugar, and stir to dissolve. Add the cold apple cider. Serve over ice.

To serve hot: Heat the apple cider in the microwave or on the stovetop and add to steeped tea and spice mixture. Serve in warm mugs with cinnamon sticks.

IS LOW IN HEME IRON AND CONTAINS	
substances that inhibit absorption of nonheme	
IRON	
	calcium
	dairy phosphate
	eggs
	phytate phosphorus
X	polyphenols tannic acid
X	chlorogenic acid
X	phenolic acid
	oxalates

(THIS RECIPE)

IRON	per serving	
	heme iron MILLIGRAMS	nonheme iron MILLIGRAMS
	0.0	0.4

Soups

Stocks or broths
Important bases for soups and sauces

Vegetable broth: With the exception of beets, when preparing vegetables such as onions, celery, including celery leaves, carrots, tomatoes, kelp, spinach, kale, etc. (wash greens thoroughly), toss ends or leftovers in stockpot filled with 14 to 16 cups of water. Add 4 to 6 crushed garlic cloves (okay to include skins), 1 teaspoon each: basil, rosemary, thyme, oregano, and salt, and ¼ teaspoon white pepper. Simmer until all vegetables are tender (about 45 minutes to 1 hour); let stand to cool. Strain the vegetables and place the broth in a glass container.

Meat stock: Bones and organ meats are rich in hemoglobin/heme iron. Prepare stock using the fatty parts of the meats rather than carcass or bony parts such as neck and back, or organ meats. Strain the broth and refrigerate so the fat congeals on top and can be removed before use in soups and sauces.

Simmer fatty boneless meat scraps in 12 to 14 cups water. Season with 1 teaspoon of salt, 1 medium whole onion, and 2 tablespoons chopped fresh parsley. Simmer uncovered for 2½ hours. Cool, remove the meat, strain the broth, and refrigerate. Discard the meat.

Chicken or turkey stock: Simmer fatty boneless white and dark chicken or turkey meat in 12 to 14 cups of water. Season with 1 teaspoon of salt, 1 medium whole onion, and 2 tablespoons chopped fresh parsley. Simmer uncovered for 2½ hours. Cool, remove and reserve the meat for soups, salads, or casseroles. Before use in soups or sauces, strain the broth and refrigerate so the fat congeals on top and can be removed before use in soups and sauces.

Seafood stock: Simmer 1 pound of favorite fish (fillet) and 1 cup cleaned and deveined raw small shrimp in 12 to 14 cups water. Season with 1 teaspoon of salt, 1 medium whole onion, celery with leaves, and 2 tablespoons chopped fresh parsley. Simmer uncovered for 2½ hours. Cool, remove the meat, strain the broth, and refrigerate. Cool the strained fish, shrimp, and seasonings, and reserve for seafood lasagna.

Cream of Broccoli Soup

Serves 8

1	**bunch fresh broccoli with stems (about 5 cups)**
4	**cups turkey or chicken broth**
1	**cup brewed tea**
	Salt to taste
4	**ounces Neufchatel cheese (cream cheese)**
1½	**cups low fat milk**
½	**cup olive oil**
2	**tablespoons butter**
½	**cup flour**
1	**cup light cream**
¼	**teaspoon nutmeg**
⅛	**teaspoon red pepper**

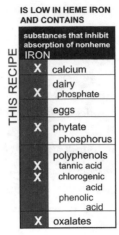

THIS RECIPE **IS LOW IN HEME IRON AND CONTAINS** substances that inhibit absorption of nonheme IRON

X	calcium
X	dairy phosphate
	eggs
X	phytate phosphorus
X X	polyphenols tannic acid chlorogenic acid phenolic acid
X	oxalates

Rinse the broccoli well. Cut and set aside about ⅔ cup of florets (tiny). Coarsely chop the stems (except for very ends) and remaining florets.

In a saucepan simmer the broccoli in the broth along with the tea and salt to taste until tender, about 15 to 20 minutes.

Cool well, then purée in a blender about 2 cups at a time (if not properly cooled the mixture can spew out when the blender is in operation). Return the puréed broccoli and broth to the warm saucepan. Add the diced Neufchatel cheese and blend. Add the milk and bring the mixture to a gentle boil over medium-high heat.

In a medium saucepan heat the oil and butter. Whisk in the flour until a paste is formed. Slowly pour the broccoli and broth mixture into the paste, whisking until smooth. Add the cream, nutmeg, and pepper. Add the florets and simmer until the florets are tender. Do not boil once the cream is added.

IRON	*per serving*	
	heme iron	nonheme iron
	MILLIGRAMS	MILLIGRAMS
	0.0	1.1

Cream of Celery and Fennel Soup

Serves 8

½	cup olive oil
1	cup finely chopped onions
1	cup chopped celery, including tops
1	cup chopped fennel, including tops
2	tablespoons butter
½	cup flour
5	cups turkey or chicken broth
1	cup brewed tea
½	cup finely chopped fresh spinach
4	ounces Neufchatel cheese, diced
1½	cups milk
1	cup light cream
1	teaspoon salt
⅛	teaspoon white pepper

THIS RECIPE IS LOW IN HEME IRON AND CONTAINS substances that inhibit absorption of nonheme IRON

X	calcium
X	dairy phosphate
	eggs
X	phytate phosphorus
X X	polyphenols tannic acid chlorogenic acid phenolic acid
X	oxalates

In a medium saucepan heat the oil and sauté the onions. Add the celery and fennel and sauté until tender.

In a separate pan heat the butter. Whisk in the flour until a paste is formed. Slowly add the broth to the paste, mixing well. Add the tea. Transfer the sautéed onion, celery, and fennel to the soup mixture. Add the spinach and Neufchatel cheese, and blend well. Add the milk and bring the mixture to a gentle boil over medium-high heat. Add the cream, salt, and pepper and heat through. Do not boil once the cream is added.

IRON	per serving heme iron MILLIGRAMS	nonheme iron MILLIGRAMS
	trace	0.4

Cream of Chicken Soup
Serves 8

½	cup olive oil
2	tablespoons butter
½	cup flour
6	cups turkey or chicken broth
1	tablespoon instant tea
1	cup pulled chicken meat
4	ounces Neufchatel cheese, diced
1½	cups low fat milk
1	cup light cream
¼	teaspoon nutmeg
⅛	teaspoon red pepper

IS LOW IN HEME IRON AND CONTAINS

THIS RECIPE	substances that inhibit absorption of nonheme IRON	
	X	calcium
	X	dairy phosphate
		eggs
	X	phytate phosphorus
	X X	polyphenols tannic acid chlorogenic acid phenolic acid
	X	oxalates

In a medium saucepan heat the oil and butter, and whisk in the flour until a paste is formed. Slowly add the broth to paste, mixing well. Add the tea, chicken, and diced Neufchatel cheese, and blend well. Add the milk and bring the mixture to a gentle boil over medium-high heat. Add the cream, nutmeg, and pepper, and heat through. Do not boil once the cream is added.

†RON	per serving	
	heme iron MILLIGRAMS	nonheme iron MILLIGRAMS
	0.4	1.1

Pepper Soup
Serves 6

2	tablespoons olive oil
1	small onion, chopped (⅓ cup)
¼	cup flour
4	cups vegetable or chicken broth
1	cup brewed tea
1	small green pepper, chopped (½ cup)
1	small red sweet pepper, chopped (½ cup)
4	ounces Neufchatel cheese, diced
1	cup milk
½	cup light cream
1	teaspoon chives
¼	teaspoon salt
¼	teaspoon black pepper
¼	teaspoon ground red pepper

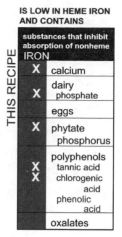

	IS LOW IN HEME IRON AND CONTAINS	
THIS RECIPE	substances that inhibit absorption of nonheme IRON	
	X	calcium
	X	dairy phosphate
		eggs
	X	phytate phosphorus
	X X	polyphenols tannic acid chlorogenic acid phenolic acid
		oxalates

In a stockpot heat the oil and sauté the onion until tender, about 20 minutes. Whisk in the flour until a paste is formed. Slowly add the broth to the paste. Add the tea, peppers, and diced Neufchatel cheese and blend. Add the milk and heat to a gentle boil. Reduce the heat and add the cream, chives, salt, and black and red peppers. Do not boil once the cream is added.

IRON	per serving heme iron MILLIGRAMS	nonheme iron MILLIGRAMS
	0.0	0.4

Potato and Leek Soup

Serves 8

6	cups russet potatoes
2	tablespoons olive oil
2	chopped leeks
1	cup finely chopped celery
7	cups vegetable stock or water
1	cup brewed tea
2	teaspoons salt
4	tablespoons dried instant mashed potatoes
1	cup milk
1	cup light cream
2	tablespoons chives
1	teaspoon black pepper

THIS RECIPE

IS LOW IN HEME IRON AND CONTAINS

	substances that inhibit absorption of nonheme IRON
X	calcium
X	dairy phosphate
	eggs
X	phytate phosphorus
X X	polyphenols tannic acid chlorogenic acid phenolic acid
	oxalates

Wash the potatoes; peel and cut in large chunks. Reserve in cold water.

In a stockpot heat the oil and sauté the leeks until tender. Add the celery and cook until tender. Add the stock (or water), tea, salt, and russet potatoes, and simmer for about 40 minutes or until the potatoes are done.

Add the instant potatoes and milk and simmer until the soup is hot. Add the cream, chives, and pepper.

IRON	per serving heme iron MILLIGRAMS	nonheme iron MILLIGRAMS
	0.0	0.77

Red Potato and Pepper Soup

Serves 8

2	tablespoons olive oil
½	cup chopped onion
½	cup diced green pepper
¼	cup pimientos, drained
1	cup brewed tea
3	cups broth
1	teaspoon salt
¼	teaspoon black pepper
12	red potatoes, washed and quartered
2	cups low fat milk
¼	to ½ cup instant mashed potatoes
½	cup sour cream
1	tablespoon chopped chives

IS LOW IN HEME IRON AND CONTAINS

THIS RECIPE

	substances that inhibit absorption of nonheme IRON
X	calcium
X	dairy phosphate
	eggs
X	phytate phosphorus
X X	polyphenols tannic acid chlorogenic acid phenolic acid
	oxalates

In a stockpot heat the oil and sauté the onion until tender, about 15 minutes.

Add the green pepper, and simmer for 5 to 6 minutes. Stir in the pimientos and heat through. Add the tea, broth, salt, pepper, and potatoes. Simmer until the potatoes are tender.

Add the milk and instant potatoes until the desired thickness. Stir in the sour cream and chives.

IRON	per serving	
	heme iron MILLIGRAMS	nonheme iron MILLIGRAMS
	0.0	0.35

Turkey Rice Soup

Serves 8

2	tablespoons olive oil
½	cup chopped onion
½	cup chopped celery
1	cup brewed tea
7	cups turkey broth
¼	cup chopped fresh spinach
⅛	cup shredded carrots
½	cup uncooked basmati rice
1	tablespoon chives
1	tablespoon salt
⅛	teaspoon black pepper
1½	cups chopped turkey meat

THIS RECIPE

IS LOW IN HEME IRON AND CONTAINS	
substances that inhibit absorption of nonheme IRON	
	calcium
	dairy phosphate
	eggs
	phytate phosphorus
X	polyphenols tannic acid chlorogenic acid phenolic acid
X	oxalates

In a stockpot heat the oil and sauté the onion until tender. Add the celery and cook for 5 minutes. Add the tea, broth, spinach, carrots, rice, chives, salt, pepper, and meat. Simmer until the rice is tender.

IRON	per serving	
	heme iron MILLIGRAMS	nonheme iron MILLIGRAMS
	0.44	2.37

Vegetable Soup

Serves 6

2	tablespoons olive oil
½	cup finely chopped onion
1	cup chopped green cabbage
½	cup coarsely chopped celery, including leaves
1	cup diced tomatoes
5	cups water
1	cup hot tea
½	can tomato paste (3 ounces)
1	teaspoon basil
2	teaspoons salt
1	teaspoon black pepper
¼	cup corn
¼	cup green peas
½	cup green beans
½	cup parsnips
½	cup diced potatoes

THIS RECIPE IS LOW IN HEME IRON AND CONTAINS

	substances that inhibit absorption of nonheme IRON
	calcium
	dairy phosphate
	eggs
	phytate phosphorus
X	polyphenols tannic acid chlorogenic acid phenolic acid
	oxalates

In a stockpot heat the oil and sauté the onion until tender. Add the cabbage and celery and cook until the cabbage is wilted. Add the diced tomatoes and bring to a boil for 10 minutes until the tomatoes are tender. Add the water, tea, tomato paste, seasonings, and all vegetables. Simmer partially covered for 1½ hours.

IRON	per serving heme iron MILLIGRAMS	nonheme iron MILLIGRAMS
	trace	0.8

Vegetable Soup with Meat
Serves 8

IS LOW IN HEME IRON AND CONTAINS	
substances that inhibit absorption of nonheme IRON	
	calcium
	dairy phosphate
	eggs
	phytate phosphorus
X	polyphenols tannic acid chlorogenic acid phenolic acid
	oxalates

THIS RECIPE

¼   cup olive oil
½   cup finely chopped onions
¾   pound trimmed veal stew meat
      Flour to coat meat
¼   cup olive oil
1   teaspoon salt
1   teaspoon black pepper
2   cups Progresso brand crushed tomatoes with sauce
2   quarts water
1   tablespoon instant coffee
1   medium potato, peeled and cubed
1   cup sliced okra
½   cup lima beans
1   cup corn

In a stockpot heat ¼ cup of olive oil and sauté the onions for about 20 minutes.

Cut the meat into large cubes. Dredge the meat in flour. Add the remaining oil to the onions, heat, and brown the meat in the hot oil. Season the cooked meat with salt and pepper. Add the tomatoes, water, coffee, and vegetables, and simmer for 1½ hours.

IRON	per serving heme iron MILLIGRAMS	nonheme iron MILLIGRAMS
	0.3	0.7

SALADS

Chicken Salad
Serves 4 to 6

3	chicken breasts plus 1 thigh/leg piece, cooked and cooled
2	quarts water
1	tablespoon instant tea
3	hard boiled eggs
¼	cup green pepper
¼	cup celery
3	tablespoons Hellman's brand reduced fat mayonnaise
1	teaspoon yellow mustard
¼	teaspoon salt
⅓	cup sweet pickle relish

THIS RECIPE

IS LOW IN HEME IRON AND CONTAINS

	substances that inhibit absorption of nonheme IRON
	calcium
X	dairy
	phosphate
	eggs
X	phytate
	phosphorus
X	polyphenols
X	tannic acid
	chlorogenic acid
	phenolic acid
	oxalates

In a stockpot simmer the chicken in the water with the instant tea for 1 hour.

Remove the chicken and place in the refrigerator to cool. Reserve the broth for other recipes.

When the chicken is completely cooled (40° to 45°F. center temperature), pull from the bone, taking care to remove all cartilage, fat, and skin. Watch for small bones. Place the chicken in a food processor and chop until coarse. Place the chopped chicken in a large mixing bowl. Chop the boiled eggs in the food processor, pulsing until coarse; add to the mixing bowl. Chop the green pepper and celery in the food processor, pulsing until coarse; add to the mixing bowl (peppers and celery will clean the egg from the bowl of processor). Add the mayo 1 tablespoon at a time, and add the yellow mustard, salt, and sweet pickle relish. It is best to combine the mixture with bare hands. Add tiny amounts of mayo until the desired consistency is reached. Refrigerate before serving.

Serve as a cold plate with pasta salad and cottage cheese.

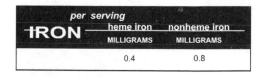

IRON	per serving	
	heme iron MILLIGRAMS	nonheme iron MILLIGRAMS
	0.4	0.8

Diet Turkey Salad

Serves 4 to 6

2	cups cold, cooked white turkey meat
¼	green pepper, cut into pieces
1	stalk celery, cut into pieces
2	tablespoons chopped onion
3	cooked egg whites
3	tablespoons Hellman's brand reduced fat mayonnaise
	Dash salt (optional)

IS LOW IN HEME IRON AND CONTAINS

THIS RECIPE	substances that inhibit absorption of nonheme IRON	
		calcium
	X	dairy phosphate
		eggs
	X	phytate phosphorus
	X X	polyphenols tannic acid chlorogenic acid phenolic acid
		oxalates

In a food processor pulse the turkey meat until chopped. Remove and set aside.

In the food processor place the green pepper, celery, and onion, and pulse until coarsely ground. Add to the turkey. In the processor chop the egg whites. Transfer to the turkey mixture. Add the mayonnaise and mix thoroughly. Season with salt to taste.

Note: Due to the vitamin C content of this recipe it is advised that the turkey salad be consumed with 2 slices of whole-wheat toast and tea or coffee as a beverage.

┼RON	*per serving*	
	heme iron MILLIGRAMS	nonheme iron MILLIGRAMS
	0.1	0.2

Broccoli Cauliflower Salad
Serves 4 to 6

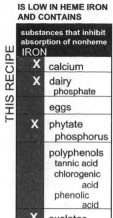

1	cup fresh broccoli florets
1	cup cauliflower florets
1	cup mayonnaise
1	tablespoon sugar
2	tablespoons apple cider vinegar
¼	cup crumbled crisp bacon
½	cup celery

In a salad dish combine the broccoli and cauliflower. In a small bowl combine the mayonnaise, sugar, and vinegar with a whisk. Pour over the broccoli and cauliflower and stir in the bacon and celery.

THIS RECIPE

IS LOW IN HEME IRON AND CONTAINS

substances that inhibit absorption of nonheme **IRON**

X	calcium
X	dairy phosphate
	eggs
X	phytate phosphorus
	polyphenols tannic acid chlorogenic acid phenolic acid
X	oxalates

IRON	per serving	
	heme iron MILLIGRAMS	nonheme iron MILLIGRAMS
	0.0	0.4

Cole Slaw

Serves 4

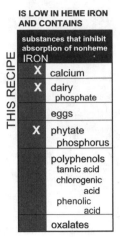

½	head cabbage	
¼	green pepper	
1	rib celery	
¼	cup sliced onion	
¼	cup sliced carrot	
½	cup mayonnaise	
¼	cup cider vinegar	
¼	teaspoon salt	
¼	cup sugar	

Wash the cabbage, cut into pieces, and place in a food processor. Pulse until finely chopped, and transfer to a large bowl. Place the green pepper, celery, onion, and carrot in the processor, and pulse until coarse. Add to the chopped cabbage.

In a separate bowl whisk together the mayonnaise, vinegar, salt, and sugar. Pour into the cabbage mixture and blend. Refrigerate until ready to serve.

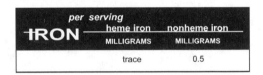

IRON	per serving	
	heme iron MILLIGRAMS	nonheme iron MILLIGRAMS
	trace	0.5

Honey Mustard
Serving size: 2 tablespoons

1	cup mayonnaise
¼	cup spicy mustard
¼	cup honey

In a small bowl combine all of the ingredients and mix well with a whisk.

Honey mustard can be used as a spread for sandwiches, a dipping sauce for vegetables or meat, or a salad dressing. Reduced fat mayonnaise can be substituted.

IRON	*per serving*	
	heme iron	nonheme iron
	MILLIGRAMS	MILLIGRAMS
	trace	0.1

Italian Dressing
Serves 4

2	tablespoons olive oil
1	tablespoon cider vinegar
¾	teaspoon salt
½	teaspoon garlic powder

In a shaker with a tight-fitting lid combine all of the ingredients. Shake until blended.

Pour onto salad for four and toss well until all lettuce is coated. The secret is in the tossing.

IRON	*per serving*	
	heme iron	nonheme iron
	MILLIGRAMS	MILLIGRAMS
	0.0	0.09

Layered Salad
Serves 6

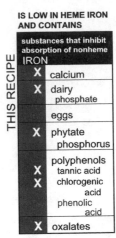

½	cup mayonnaise
1	cup sour cream
3	cups chopped lettuce (romaine and iceberg work best)
⅔	cup chopped raw cauliflower
⅔	cup chopped raw broccoli
½	cup frozen small peas
½	cup coarsely chopped walnuts
4	spring onions, washed, trimmed, and diced (reserve tops)
½	cup finely chopped celery
2	cups shredded sharp Cheddar cheese
6	strips crisp bacon or Webb's Faux Bacon (see recipe on page 164)
	Salt to taste

In a small bowl mix the mayonnaise and sour cream to create a sauce.

In a glass dish alternate layers of lettuce, cauliflower, broccoli, peas, walnuts, onions, celery, sauce, cheese, and bacon, ending with cheese and bacon as the final layers. Sprinkle salt as desired onto the lettuce layers. Refrigerate until serving.

IRON	per serving	
	heme iron MILLIGRAMS	nonheme iron MILLIGRAMS
	trace	1.26

Low Calorie Herb and Cucumber Dressing

Makes about ¾ cup; serves 6

1	small pickling cucumber, washed and cut in chunks
½	cup Hellman's brand low fat mayo
¼	cup cider vinegar
¾	teaspoon salt
½	teaspoon garlic powder
1	teaspoon chives
½	teaspoon parsley
¼	teaspoon marjoram
¼	teaspoon oregano

THIS RECIPE	IS LOW IN HEME IRON AND CONTAINS	
	substances that inhibit absorption of nonheme IRON	
		calcium
		dairy phosphate
		eggs
		phytate phosphorus
		polyphenols tannic acid chlorogenic acid phenolic acid
	X	oxalates

In a food processor pulse the cucumber until finely chopped. Add the mayonnaise and mix well. Add the cider vinegar and remaining ingredients, and blend well.

IRON	per serving	
	heme iron MILLIGRAMS	nonheme iron MILLIGRAMS
	trace	0.01

Macaroni Salad
Serves 8

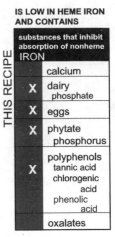

IS LOW IN HEME IRON
AND CONTAINS

THIS RECIPE	substances that inhibit absorption of nonheme IRON	
		calcium
	X	dairy phosphate
	X	eggs
	X	phytate phosphorus
	X	polyphenols tannic acid chlorogenic acid phenolic acid
		oxalates

½ cup mayonnaise

2 tablespoons sugar

3 tablespoons cider vinegar

½ teaspoon salt

2 quarts water

½ teaspoon salt

1 tablespoon instant tea

2 cups dry elbow macaroni

¼ cup finely chopped onion

½ cup finely chopped celery

2 boiled eggs, chopped

In a small bowl whisk together the mayonnaise, sugar, vinegar, and ½ teaspoon of salt.

In a stockpot bring the water to a boil. Add ½ teaspoon of salt, the tea, and macaroni, and cook for 10 minutes. Drain and rinse.

While the noodles are still warm add the mayonnaise mixture, onion, celery, and eggs. Cover and refrigerate for several hours; overnight is best.

IRON	per serving heme iron MILLIGRAMS	nonheme iron MILLIGRAMS
	trace	0.67

Oil Free Salad Dressing

Makes about 2 cups; serving size 2 tablespoons

½   cup cold brewed tea
1   teaspoon Knox unflavored gelatin
1   cup boiling water
¼   cup red wine vinegar
1   tablespoon spicy mustard
½   teaspoon paprika
1   teaspoon garlic powder
1   teaspoon dried parsley flakes
1   teaspoon salt
¼   teaspoon black pepper

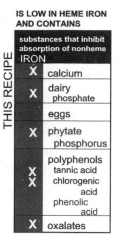

THIS RECIPE	IS LOW IN HEME IRON AND CONTAINS	
	substances that inhibit absorption of nonheme IRON	
	X	calcium
	X	dairy phosphate
		eggs
	X	phytate phosphorus
	X X	polyphenols tannic acid chlorogenic acid phenolic acid
	X	oxalates

In a blender combine the cold tea and gelatin. Add the boiling water and process at low speed until the gelatin is completely dissolved. Add the remaining ingredients and continue blending on low speed until combined. Place in a glass jar with a lid and refrigerate.

Shake well before serving.

IRON	per serving	
	heme iron MILLIGRAMS	nonheme iron MILLIGRAMS
	trace	0.8

Pasta Salad
Serves 10 to 12

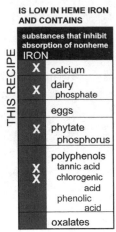

DRESSING:

2	tablespoons olive oil
1	tablespoon cider vinegar
1	teaspoon salt
1	teaspoon garlic powder
¼	teaspoon oregano
¼	teaspoon basil

SALAD:

1	16-ounce box whole-wheat rotini pasta
2	quarts water
1	tablespoon instant tea
1	teaspoon salt
2	pickling cucumbers, cubed
1	cup tomato relish
6	ounces Provolone cheese, cut into small cubes
⅔	cup sliced black olives
4	ounces hard salami, cut into thin strips
½	cup Parmesan cheese

In a shaker combine the olive oil, cider vinegar, and remaining ingredients. Shake until well combined.

In a large pot cook the pasta in the water and tea with salt until tender.

Drain, rinse, and toss with dressing. Add the cucumbers and tomato relish, and toss. Add the Provolone, olives, salami, and Parmesan. Chill before serving.

Note: ¼ cup Kraft Zesty Italian is a good substitute.

IRON	per serving	
	heme iron MILLIGRAMS	nonheme iron MILLIGRAMS
	0.5	0.56

Potato Salad

Serves 10 to 12

3	pounds red skinned potatoes
2	quarts water
1	teaspoon salt
1	tablespoon instant tea
½	cup mayonnaise
1	tablespoon yellow mustard
¼	cup sugar
¼	cup apple cider vinegar
¼	cup finely chopped onion
½	cup finely chopped celery
2	chopped hard-boiled eggs

THIS RECIPE IS LOW IN HEME IRON AND CONTAINS

substances that inhibit absorption of nonheme IRON

	calcium
X	dairy phosphate
	eggs
X	phytate phosphorus
X X	polyphenols tannic acid chlorogenic acid phenolic acid
	oxalates

Rinse the potatoes. In a stockpot boil the potatoes in salted water with the tea for about 40 minutes.

In a small bowl combine the mayonnaise, mustard, sugar, and vinegar.

Drain and cut each potato in half. Place in a salad bowl. While still warm, add the onion, celery, eggs, and mayonnaise mixture. Combine thoroughly and refrigerate before serving.

IRON per serving

heme iron MILLIGRAMS	nonheme iron MILLIGRAMS
0.0	0.5

Tuna Salad
Serves 2

1	**2.5-ounce can white water-packed tuna**
1	**boiled egg**
2	**tablespoons finely chopped onion**
4	**tablespoons finely chopped celery**
2	**tablespoons mayonnaise**

Place the tuna in a food processor and pulse until coarsely ground. Transfer the tuna to a medium bowl. Add to the processor one hard-boiled egg. Pulse until coarsely chopped. Place the egg in the bowl with the tuna. In the processor add the onion and celery, and pulse until finely chopped. Combine with the tuna and egg.

Add mayonnaise a bit at a time.

This recipe contains a moderate amount of iron. Drinking tea with this recipe is recommended.

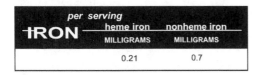

IRON	per serving heme iron MILLIGRAMS	nonheme iron MILLIGRAMS
	0.21	0.7

Applesauce Bread

Makes 2 loaves

1	cup coarsely grated apples
2	tablespoons apple juice
1½	cups oat blend flour
¼	teaspoon salt
1	teaspoon baking soda
1	cup light brown sugar
1	cup apple butter
1	egg, lightly beaten
½	cup buttermilk
½	cup chopped English walnuts

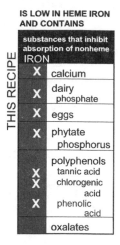

IS LOW IN HEME IRON AND CONTAINS

THIS RECIPE

substances that inhibit absorption of nonheme IRON	
X	calcium
X	dairy phosphate
X	eggs
X	phytate phosphorus
X X	polyphenols tannic acid chlorogenic acid
X	phenolic acid
	oxalates

In a small bowl sprinkle the apples with apple juice. Set aside.

In a medium bowl sift together the flour, salt, and baking soda.

In a large bowl blend the sugar, apple butter, and egg. Alternate adding dry ingredients and buttermilk to the applesauce mixture until all ingredients are thoroughly combined. Fold in the apples and walnuts.

Spray 2 loaf pans with vegetable spray. Divide the batter evenly among both pans. Bake at 350° for 55 minutes. Check for doneness by inserting a thin knife blade into the center. The knife blade will come out clean if the center is done. Dump the loaf onto a cooling rack and let cool until set enough to slice and serve warm.

IRON	per serving heme iron MILLIGRAMS	nonheme iron MILLIGRAMS
	0.0	0.4

Blueberry Coffee Cake
Serves 8

2 cups oat blend flour
1 teaspoon baking soda
2 teaspoons baking powder
½ teaspoon salt
4 tablespoons olive oil
¾ cup light brown sugar
1 egg
½ cup buttermilk
2 cups fresh blueberries, rinsed and drained

CRUMB TOPPING:
4 tablespoons butter
¼ cup oat flour
½ cup light brown sugar
½ teaspoon cinnamon

IS LOW IN HEME IRON AND CONTAINS	
substances that inhibit absorption of nonheme IRON	
X	calcium
X	dairy phosphate
X	eggs
X	phytate phosphorus
X	polyphenols tannic acid chlorogenic acid phenolic acid
	oxalates

THIS RECIPE

In a medium bowl sift together the flour, baking soda, baking powder, and salt. Set aside.

In a large bowl blend the oil and sugar together. Add the egg and buttermilk to the sugar mixture. Blend in the dry ingredients. Fold in the blueberries. Pour the batter into an oiled and floured 9-inch square baking dish.

Prepare the topping: In a small bowl blend the butter into the flour, sugar, and cinnamon with a pastry cutter. Sprinkle the crumb mixture over the surface. Bake at 375° for 40 to 45 minutes.

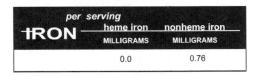

IRON	per serving	
	heme iron MILLIGRAMS	nonheme iron MILLIGRAMS
	0.0	0.76

Bran Muffins
Makes 12

1¼ cups Nabisco brand bite-size shredded wheat with bran
1   cup brewed hot coffee
1   cup oat blend flour
2½ teaspoons baking soda
½   teaspoon salt
½   cup brown sugar
2   eggs, lightly beaten
½   cup applesauce
½   cup Faux Molasses (see recipe on page 216)
½   cup buttermilk
1   cup chopped English walnuts

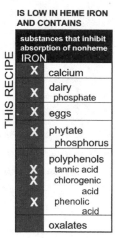

THIS RECIPE	IS LOW IN HEME IRON AND CONTAINS	
	substances that inhibit absorption of nonheme **IRON**	
	X	calcium
	X	dairy phosphate
	X	eggs
	X	phytate phosphorus
	X X	polyphenols tannic acid chlorogenic acid
	X	phenolic acid
		oxalates

Preheat the oven to 375°. Spray a 12-cup muffin pan with vegetable spray.

In a large bowl soak the cereal in coffee about 15 minutes.

In a separate bowl sift together the flour, soda, and salt. Set aside.

In a medium bowl mix the brown sugar and eggs together. Add the applesauce and faux molasses to the egg-sugar mixture, and blend well. Add to the cereal and mix well. Alternate adding milk and flour to the cereal mixture. Fold in the nuts. Scoop enough batter into each muffin cup to fill about two-thirds full. Bake for 17 minutes or until done.

Cool and refrigerate any remaining muffins. Warm in the microwave for 20 to 30 seconds before serving.

IRON	per serving heme iron MILLIGRAMS	nonheme iron MILLIGRAMS
	0.0	1.0

Buttermilk Biscuits
Serves 8

1½	cups oat blend flour
½	teaspoon salt
¼	teaspoon baking soda
½	teaspoon baking powder
¼	cup Crisco brand shortening
1	cup buttermilk

	IS LOW IN HEME IRON AND CONTAINS
	substances that inhibit absorption of nonheme IRON
X	calcium
X	dairy phosphate
X	eggs
X	phytate phosphorus
	polyphenols tannic acid chlorogenic acid phenolic acid
	oxalates

THIS RECIPE

In a medium bowl sift the flour, salt, baking soda, and baking powder together and pile onto a pastry cloth. Cut the shortening into the flour until blended. Shape the dough into a pile. Make a well in the center. Slowly pour the buttermilk into the center, blending the edges from the outside into the milk. Continue adding milk and blending flour. The dough will be wet. Flour a rolling pin and roll out the dough very gently until about 1½ inches thick. Flour a biscuit cutter (the rim of a sturdy small glass can be used as a cutter) and cut out biscuits. Place close together in a shallow ungreased baking dish. Bake at 450° for about 8 to 10 minutes until golden brown on top.

┼RON	*per serving* heme iron MILLIGRAMS	nonheme iron MILLIGRAMS
	0.0	0.3

Coffee Can Apple-Zucchini Bread
Makes 4 "loaves"

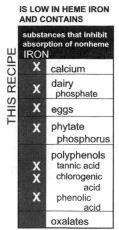

IS LOW IN HEME IRON AND CONTAINS

THIS RECIPE	substances that inhibit absorption of nonheme IRON	
	X	calcium
	X	dairy phosphate
	X	eggs
	X	phytate phosphorus
	X X X	polyphenols tannic acid chlorogenic acid phenolic acid
		oxalates

3	cups oat blend flour
2	teaspoons baking soda
1	teaspoon salt
1	teaspoon nutmeg
1	teaspoon cinnamon
½	teaspoon ground cloves
2	cups light brown sugar
⅔	cup olive oil
⅔	cup buttermilk
1	egg
½	cup chopped apples
½	cup chopped zucchini
½	cup chopped English walnuts

Preheat the oven to 350°. Wash and completely dry four 1-pound coffee cans. Oil and flour the insides of cans. Set aside.

In a large bowl combine the flour, baking soda, salt, nutmeg, cinnamon, cloves, and brown sugar. Add the oil, buttermilk, and egg, and mix well. Fold in the apples, zucchini, and walnuts. Divide the batter equally among the 4 cans. Bake at 350° for 55 to 60 minutes. Check the center for doneness.

Allow to cool before removing the bread from the cans. Each should slip out easily; if not, slide a thin knife blade between the inside of the can and the bread.

Remove, cool further, wrap, and refrigerate.

IRON	*per serving*	
	heme iron MILLIGRAMS	nonheme iron MILLIGRAMS
	0.0	0.9

Corn Bread

Serves 6 to 8

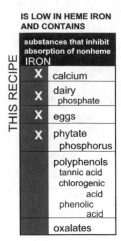

¼	cup olive oil
1	cups Yelton's brand cornmeal
1	cup oat blend flour
4	teaspoons baking powder
1	teaspoon baking soda
½	teaspoon salt
1	egg
1½	cups buttermilk

Pour the oil in an 8-inch square glass baking dish. Heat the oil in a 450° oven.

In a medium bowl mix the cornmeal, flour, baking powder, baking soda, and salt. In a separate bowl mix the egg and buttermilk. Add the dry ingredients to the buttermilk mixture. When completely blended add the hot oil to the mixture. Stir and pour the batter into the heated baking dish. Bake for 15 minutes.

IRON	*per serving*	
	heme iron	nonheme iron
	MILLIGRAMS	MILLIGRAMS
	0.0	0.4

Dill Weed Bread

Makes 2 loaves (about 20 slices)

2½	cups whole-wheat flour
2	tablespoons sugar
1	teaspoon salt
¼	teaspoon baking soda
1	package dry yeast
¼	cup warm coffee
1	tablespoon olive oil
1	egg
1	cup buttermilk
2	tablespoons dill
1	tablespoon instant onion

THIS RECIPE IS LOW IN HEME IRON AND CONTAINS

substances that inhibit absorption of nonheme IRON	
X	calcium
X	dairy phosphate
X	eggs
X	phytate phosphorus
X X	polyphenols tannic acid chlorogenic acid phenolic acid
X	oxalates

In a medium bowl sift together the flour, sugar, salt, and baking soda.

In a large bowl soften the yeast with the warm coffee. Add the oil.

In a medium bowl lightly beat the egg, and add the buttermilk. Add the dill and onion.

Alternately add the dry ingredients and buttermilk mixture to the coffee mixture. The dough will become stiff. Turn out onto a pastry cloth and knead. Place in a large greased glass bowl. Cover with a tea towel and allow to rise until doubled in size, about 1 hour.

Turn out onto a pastry cloth. Punch down, knead, and divide into 2 loaves. Place in 2 well-greased and floured loaf pans. Cover and allow to rise for 45 minutes.

Bake at 350° for 45 to 50 minutes.

IRON	per serving heme iron MILLIGRAMS	nonheme iron MILLIGRAMS
	0.0	0.6

Herb Wheat Rolls
Makes 36 rolls

	substances that inhibit absorption of nonheme IRON
THIS RECIPE	
X	calcium
X	dairy phosphate
X	eggs
X	phytate phosphorus
X X	polyphenols tannic acid chlorogenic acid phenolic acid
X	oxalates

1	cup warm coffee
2	packages dry yeast
2	cups scalded low fat milk
7¼	cups whole-wheat flour
2	teaspoons salt
½	teaspoon dried basil
½	teaspoon dried rosemary
½	teaspoon dried marjoram
½	teaspoon dried oregano
½	cup olive oil
2	eggs, lightly beaten

In a large bowl pour the warm coffee over the yeast.

Pour the scalded milk in a separate bowl and add a small amount of flour (about 1 cup). Stir in the salt, herbs, and oil. Then add the yeast-coffee mixture. Add flour slowly, then eggs, until all is combined. The dough will no longer stick to the edges of the bowl when properly combined. Turn the dough out onto a floured pastry cloth and let stand for 10 minutes.

Knead until elastic and smooth. Lightly oil the sides of a large bowl. Place the dough in a bowl, and cover with a tea towel. Let rise until doubled in size, about 1 hour.

Punch down, and shape into rolls. Allow to rise again for about 40 minutes.

Bake at 425° for about 10 to 12 minutes until the tops are golden brown.

IRON	*per serving* heme iron MILLIGRAMS	nonheme iron MILLIGRAMS
	0.0	0.8

Onion-Herb Corn Bread
Serves 6 to 8

¼	cup olive oil
2	tablespoons finely chopped onion
1	cup Yelton's brand cornmeal
1	cup oat blend flour
4	teaspoons baking powder
1	teaspoon baking soda
1	teaspoon dried basil
1	teaspoon dried oregano
½	teaspoon salt
1	egg
1½	cups buttermilk

IS LOW IN HEME IRON AND CONTAINS

THIS RECIPE	substances that inhibit absorption of nonheme IRON	
	X	calcium
	X	dairy phosphate
	X	eggs
	X	phytate phosphorus
		polyphenols tannic acid chlorogenic acid phenolic acid
	X	oxalates

In a skillet heat the oil and sauté the onion until tender. Set aside.

In a medium bowl mix the cornmeal, flour, baking powder, baking soda, basil, oregano, and salt.

In a large bowl mix together the egg and buttermilk.

Pour the oil and onion in a glass baking dish. Heat in a 450° oven and heat for 5 to 7 minutes.

Meanwhile add the dry ingredients to the liquid mixture. When completely blended add the hot oil and onions to the batter. Stir and pour the batter into a heated baking dish. Bake for 15 minutes.

IRON	per serving heme iron MILLIGRAMS	nonheme iron MILLIGRAMS
	0.0	0.4

Peanut Butter Banana Muffins

Makes 12 muffins

1	cup whole-wheat flour
¾	cup Quaker brand oats
1	tablespoon baking powder
1	teaspoon baking soda
½	teaspoon salt
½	cup brown sugar
½	cup Jif brand peanut butter
1	banana, well mashed
1	tablespoon apple juice
1	teaspoon vanilla extract
2	tablespoons olive oil
1	egg
1	cup buttermilk

TOPPING:

¼	cup oats
¼	cup wheat flour
2	tablespoons butter, melted
2	tablespoons brown sugar

THIS RECIPE

IS LOW IN HEME IRON AND CONTAINS

substances that inhibit absorption of nonheme IRON	
X	calcium
X	dairy phosphate
X	eggs
X	phytate phosphorus
X	polyphenols tannic acid chlorogenic acid
X	phenolic acid
	oxalates

Spray a 12-cup muffin pan generously with vegetable spray. In a medium bowl sift together the flour, oats, baking powder, baking soda, and salt.

In a large bowl mix together the brown sugar, peanut butter, banana, apple juice, vanilla, and oil. Blend the egg and buttermilk, and add to the sugar mixture. Add the dry ingredients and mix just until moistened. Pour the batter evenly into the muffin pan.

In a small bowl combine the topping ingredients and mix until crumbly. Sprinkle the top of each muffin with the topping. Bake at 375° for 18 minutes.

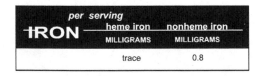

IRON	per serving	
	heme iron MILLIGRAMS	nonheme iron MILLIGRAMS
	trace	0.8

SANDWICHES

Legend is that the sandwich was invented in the mid 1700s by an English nobleman whose title was the Earl of Sandwich, so derived from the name of the town Sandwich. It seems the Earl requested that a slab of meat be served between two slices of bread, which was a novel approach to eating one's dinner. His motive seemed to be driven by his love of playing cards. Eating in this way he could have one hand free so that he could hold his cards in the other. Another legend is that an English housewife weary of the consequences of greasy fingers and the constant cleaning associated with mealtime, slathered a creamy concoction we know today as mayonnaise onto two slices of bread, which also held a slab of meat.

In any event, bread is a necessary component of the traditional American sandwich, which today can be made in a variety of ways. Pockets, wraps, shells, and interesting breads such as Ezekiel and other multigrain breads add fiber to the diet and uniqueness of taste and texture.

Bread dates back to ancient Egypt, where more than four thousand years ago bakers discovered the qualities of yeast; until then bread was unleavened. Bread was often made in the home using wholegrain flours, although bakeries were commonplace throughout Europe and the USA. During Civil War times there were more than 2,000 bakeries in America. It was also during this time that the invention of specialized milling equipment allowed commercial bakeries to refine flour and produce lighter breads. After World War II few homemakers made bread at home; instead they purchased commercially produced breads that by now lined the shelves of grocery stores. For aesthetics commercial bakeries refined the grains, milling away the bran portion of the wheat. They spun air into the dough to give it a light and delicate texture and they added preservatives to extend the shelf life of the product. In the 1940s bakers began to add fortificants such as iron to commercially made bread. Americans consumed this type of bread for decades until the benefits of consuming whole grains led to the restoration of whole-grain breads in great variety. However, fortificants such as iron continue to be added to most commercially produced breads.

All breads contain nonheme iron, some more than others, especially those heavily fortified with iron. Whole-grain breads are high in insoluble fiber (part of phytates), which causes this iron to have low bioavailability. However, two fortificants that will soon make their way into our food supply, Ferrochel and EDTA-Fe, have the ability to override the iron-inhibitory capabilities of fiber. Individuals with iron-loading conditions will need to pay special attention to foods fortified with these substances.

Meanwhile, enjoy sandwiches made with breads such as bagels, whole grains, and pita pockets, and try to drink tea or coffee with sandwiches.

Bagel: a roll made of yeast dough that is rolled and twisted into a doughnut shape, dropped into boil water to swell, and then is baked.

Biscuit: made of lard or vegetable shortening such as Crisco, which is cut into flour, to which buttermilk is added.

English muffin: rolled dough cut into circles and sprinkled with cornmeal are cooked on a very hot iron skillet, which accounts for its higher than baked bread iron content.

Ezekiel bread: called the Bible bread, it is an ancient bread that is low in gluten. It is made with sprouted grains, which include wheat, smelt, millet, barley, lentil, and soy flour. This bread also contains soya lecithin, which is thought to aid in the control of low-density cholesterol.

French or Italian bread: crusty bread with soft, airy center

Kaiser roll: same texture as French or Italian bread except in a roll form and usually topped with poppy seed. Also referred to as hard roll.

Millet bread: a good alternative grain to those who are allergic to wheat. It contains no gluten.

Pita pocket: an ancient flatbread common in the Mediterranean.

Pumpernickel: a coarse dark bread made with unsifted rye, also called Westphalian rye, popular in Germany.

Rye: having its distinct flavor derived from caraway seed rye bread is another German bread.

Taco shell: made from corn.

Tortilla: flat unleavened corn cake common in Mexico.

White: usually made from refined white flours, which does not contain the bran portion of the grain.

Whole-wheat: contains the bran portion of the grain.

Some sandwiches in *Cooking with Less Iron* are from the roster of favorites served in my restaurant. To add novelty to the menu, most of the sandwiches were given silly names based on the names of famous people. This list includes Jose Felisalami, Veggie Jackson, Nickolettuce and Aleggsandria, Ike 'n' Tina Tuna, and Frankenstein's Muenster. Some sandwiches were named after favorite songs such as "Don't Go Bacon My Heart," "Fool's Russian In," and "Pig O My Heart."

Bean, Rice, and Cheese Pita
Serves 2

½	cup pinto beans (cooked according to recipe on page 177)
½	cup wild rice, cooked according to recipe with tea
½	cup shredded Cheddar cheese
2	pita pockets
4	fresh spinach leaves
¼	cup chopped spring onion
¼	cup reduced fat mayonnaise

In a medium bowl combine the beans, rice, and cheese. Line pita pockets with spinach leaves, and spoon the bean mixture into the pocket. Add onion and squirt mayonnaise into the sandwich.

THIS RECIPE	IS LOW IN HEME IRON AND CONTAINS
	substances that inhibit absorption of nonheme IRON
X	calcium
X	dairy phosphate
	eggs
X	phytate phosphorus
X	polyphenols tannic acid chlorogenic acid phenolic acid
X	oxalates

IRON	per serving	
	heme iron	nonheme iron
	MILLIGRAMS	MILLIGRAMS
	0.0	1.3

Chicken Fajita

Serves 4

2	**boneless, skinless chicken breasts, cut into narrow strips**
¼	**cup water**
1	**teaspoon instant tea**
½	**teaspoon red pepper**
½	**teaspoon salt**
1	**tablespoon olive oil**
1	**cup thinly sliced onion**
1	**cup thinly sliced green pepper**
4	**tortilla or pita pockets**

IS LOW IN HEME IRON AND CONTAINS

THIS RECIPE

	substances that inhibit absorption of nonheme IRON
X	calcium
X	dairy phosphate
	eggs
X	phytate phosphorus
X X	polyphenols tannic acid chlorogenic acid phenolic acid
	oxalates

In a stockpot simmer the chicken in water and tea until done and the meat begins to brown around the edges. Sprinkle with red pepper and salt. Remove the meat and set aside. In a skillet heat the oil and sauté the onion for 15 minutes until tender. Add the green pepper and continue cooking until the pepper is tender. Add the meat to the pan with the pepper and onion. Heat through. Divide portions evenly to fill 4 warm tortillas or pita pockets.

IRON	*per serving* heme iron MILLIGRAMS	nonheme iron MILLIGRAMS
	0.2	0.9

Cucumber Club

Serves 1

1	ounce Neufchatel cheese
3	slices whole-wheat bread
4	to 5 slices cucumber
1	onion, thinly sliced
1	slice tomato
2	slices avocado
	Pinch alfalfa sprouts

THIS RECIPE	IS LOW IN HEME IRON AND CONTAINS	
	substances that inhibit absorption of nonheme IRON	
	X	calcium
	X	dairy phosphate
		eggs
	X	phytate phosphorus
	X	polyphenols tannic acid chlorogenic acid phenolic acid
	X	oxalates

Spread Neufchatel onto 2 slices of bread. On one slice place cucumbers and onion. Stack the next slice of bread, which is spread with Neufchatel. Layer with avocado, tomato, and sprouts. Top with the last piece of bread. Cut diagonally and secure with toothpicks.

IRON	per serving heme iron MILLIGRAMS	nonheme iron MILLIGRAMS
	0.0	3.9

Eggplant Pocket
Serves 2

2   tablespoons olive oil
½   cup chopped onion
½   cup chopped pepper
½   cup raw eggplant strips
     Pinch oregano
½   cup brewed tea
1   cup Marinara Sauce (see recipe on page 204)

In a skillet heat the oil and sauté the onion until tender. Add the
pepper, eggplant, oregano, and tea, and simmer until tender. Add
the marinara sauce and simmer uncovered for 20 minutes. Spoon the mixture into pita
pockets. Serve warm.

	IS LOW IN HEME IRON AND CONTAINS	
THIS RECIPE	substances that inhibit absorption of nonheme IRON	
		calcium
	X	dairy phosphate
		eggs
	X	phytate phosphorus
	X	polyphenols tannic acid chlorogenic acid phenolic acid
	X	oxalates

IRON	per serving heme iron MILLIGRAMS	nonheme iron MILLIGRAMS
	0.0	0.5

Ham with Salami and Mustard Sauce
Serves 2

4   tablespoons reduced fat mayonnaise
1   tablespoon spicy mustard
2   pita pockets
1   ounce thinly sliced hard salami
2   ounces thinly sliced deli ham
2   ounces Swiss cheese, cut julienne style

In a small bowl mix the mayonnaise and mustard and place in a
squeeze bottle. Stuff the pita pockets with meat and cheese and
squirt the sauce into the pockets.

	IS LOW IN HEME IRON AND CONTAINS	
THIS RECIPE	substances that inhibit absorption of nonheme IRON	
	X	calcium
	X	dairy phosphate
		eggs
	X	phytate phosphorus
		polyphenols tannic acid chlorogenic acid phenolic acid
		oxalates

IRON	per serving heme iron MILLIGRAMS	nonheme iron MILLIGRAMS
	0.2	0.5

Hamburger with Cheese and Onion

Serves 1

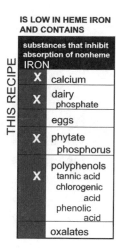

	IS LOW IN HEME IRON AND CONTAINS
THIS RECIPE	substances that inhibit absorption of nonheme IRON
X	calcium
X	dairy phosphate
	eggs
X	phytate phosphorus
X	polyphenols tannic acid chlorogenic acid phenolic acid
	oxalates

2	ounces ground beef
2	ounces ground turkey
1	tablespoon olive oil
¼	cup finely chopped onions
¼	cup brewed tea
	Salt and pepper
1	slice creamy havarti cheese
1	hamburger bun

In a medium bowl mix the beef and turkey and form into a patty.

In a small skillet heat the oil and sauté the onions. Add the meat and tea. Season with salt and pepper. Simmer until the liquid evaporates.

Place cheese on top of the meat and cover so the cheese will melt. Toast the hamburger bun and place the patty and onions on the bottom half of the bun. Add mustard and catsup to the top bun as desired.

Note: If lettuce and tomato are eaten with this sandwich, drink tea or coffee.

By mixing beef with turkey, the iron content is reduced by nearly a milligram, creating a low heme iron version of the classic American favorite—the hamburger. This recipe also contains tannins, phytate phosphorus, phosphates, calcium.

IRON	per serving heme iron MILLIGRAMS	nonheme iron MILLIGRAMS
	0.5	3.4

Hot Dogs Deluxe

Serves 1

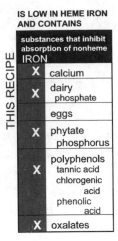

IS LOW IN HEME IRON
AND CONTAINS

THIS RECIPE	substances that inhibit absorption of nonheme IRON	
	X	calcium
	X	dairy phosphate
		eggs
	X	phytate phosphorus
	X	polyphenols tannic acid chlorogenic acid phenolic acid
	X	oxalates

2	turkey hot dogs, split lengthwise
¼	cup brewed tea
¼	cup hot dog chili sauce
1	side of ⅓ loaf of French bread
2	tablespoons reduced fat mayonnaise
	Garlic powder
	Pinch finely chopped fresh parsley
1	teaspoon spicy mustard
1	teaspoon finely chopped onion
¼	cup coleslaw
1	teaspoon catsup
2	slices Muenster cheese

In a skillet sear the hot dogs over high heat. Add the tea and simmer for 10 minutes. Remove the meat from the pan and set aside. In a saucepan warm the chili sauce.

Split the bread down the center and cover with mayonnaise. Sprinkle with garlic powder and parsley. Place under the broiler until toasted. Remove from the oven but leave the broiler on. Spread mustard onto the toasted surface. Place hot dogs cut side down on the bread. Top with chili sauce, onion, slaw, catsup, and cheese. Place under the broiler long enough to melt the cheese.

IRON	*per serving*	
	heme iron MILLIGRAMS	nonheme iron MILLIGRAMS
	0.4	0.9

Hot Dogs with Chili
Serves 8

1	tablespoon olive oil
¼	cup finely chopped onion
1	pound ground turkey
1	teaspoon salt
½	teaspoon red pepper
1	teaspoon cumin
3	tablespoons tomato paste
3	tablespoons catsup
½	cup hot coffee
8	turkey hot dogs
8	whole-wheat hot dog buns

IS LOW IN HEME IRON AND CONTAINS

THIS RECIPE

substances that inhibit absorption of nonheme IRON	
	calcium
	dairy phosphate
	eggs
	phytate phosphorus
X	polyphenols tannic acid chlorogenic acid phenolic acid
	oxalates

In a skillet heat the oil and sauté the onion until tender. Add the ground turkey, seasonings, tomato paste, catsup, and coffee. Simmer for 20 to 30 minutes.

Heat the hot dogs. Place on the buns and top with sauce.

Tip: Place the hot dog with bun and sauce on a tray in a warm oven (275°) for 10 minutes. This steams the bun and brings out the flavor of the chili sauce. Top with your choice of fresh chopped onions, kraut, mustard, and catsup. Serve with funny fries or red potato salad, chocolate–cream cheese brownies, and iced tea.

IRON	per serving	
	heme iron MILLIGRAMS	nonheme iron MILLIGRAMS
	0.26	0.5

Omelet Sandwich
Serves 2

2	slices Canadian bacon
½	cup brewed tea
2	tablespoons olive oil
½	cup finely chopped onion
¼	cup chopped green pepper
¼	cup chopped fresh tomato
	Salt and pepper to taste
3	eggs, lightly beaten
½	cup Muenster Cheese
2	bagels, split and toasted

THIS RECIPE IS LOW IN HEME IRON AND CONTAINS substances that inhibit absorption of nonheme IRON

X	calcium
X	dairy phosphate
X	eggs
X	phytate phosphorus
X	polyphenols tannic acid chlorogenic acid phenolic acid
	oxalates

In a hot skillet sear the Canadian bacon. Add the tea and cook until the liquid evaporates. Remove the meat, cut into thin strips, and set aside. Add oil to the pan and sauté the onion until tender. Add the pepper and tomato and simmer. Season with salt and pepper. Add the beaten eggs and ham, and cook until the eggs are solid. Sprinkle the cheese over the eggs, cover, and turn off the heat. Let stand for 4 to 5 minutes until the cheese melts. Divide the omelet in half and serve on toasted bagels. Can be served open-faced on one half of a toasted bagel.

IRON	per serving heme iron MILLIGRAMS	nonheme iron MILLIGRAMS
	0.3	0.6

Open-Faced Hot Ham and Cheese
Serves 1

1	slice rye bread with caraway seed, lightly toasted
1	thin slice tomato
1	cluster broccoli florets (steamed in microwave)
3	ounces shaved ham
¼	cup cheese sauce

Place the toast on a plate. Add the tomato slice, then broccoli, and pile the ham on top. Heat in the microwave for 1 minute. Cover with hot cheese sauce.

Note: Steaming broccoli will destroy some of the vitamin C but not the beta carotene content. Drinking tea with this entrée is recommended.

THIS RECIPE IS LOW IN HEME IRON AND CONTAINS

substances that inhibit absorption of nonheme IRON

X	calcium
X	dairy phosphate
	eggs
X	phytate phosphorus
X	polyphenols tannic acid chlorogenic acid phenolic acid
	oxalates

IRON	per serving	
	heme iron MILLIGRAMS	nonheme iron MILLIGRAMS
	0.25	1.6

Pimiento Cheese Spread on Rye
Makes 2 cups

1	7-ounce jar pimientos, sliced and drained
8	ounces Neufchatel cheese
10	ounces extra sharp Cheddar cheese, shredded
⅛	teaspoon red pepper (about 6 or 7 shakes)

In a food processor place the pimiento, and pulse 3 to 4 times. Add the Neufchatel and pulse until the pimiento is blended. Add the shredded Cheddar and blend. Season with red pepper.

Spread on rye bread and serve.

THIS RECIPE IS LOW IN HEME IRON AND CONTAINS

substances that inhibit absorption of nonheme IRON

	calcium
X	dairy phosphate
	eggs
X	phytate phosphorus
X X	polyphenols tannic acid chlorogenic acid phenolic acid
	oxalates

IRON	per serving	
	heme iron MILLIGRAMS	nonheme iron MILLIGRAMS
	trace	1.8

Sausage and Peppers

Serves 4

<table>
<tr><td colspan="2">IS LOW IN HEME IRON AND CONTAINS</td></tr>
<tr><td></td><td>substances that inhibit absorption of nonheme IRON</td></tr>
<tr><td></td><td>calcium</td></tr>
<tr><td></td><td>dairy phosphate</td></tr>
<tr><td></td><td>eggs</td></tr>
<tr><td>X</td><td>phytate phosphorus</td></tr>
<tr><td>X</td><td>polyphenols tannic acid chlorogenic acid phenolic acid</td></tr>
<tr><td></td><td>oxalates</td></tr>
</table>

THIS RECIPE

¼	cup olive oil
1	cup thinly sliced onion
½	cup julienne-cut strips green bell pepper
½	pound mild turkey sausage, cut into 2-inch pieces and split
½	pound hot Italian sausage, cut into 2-inch pieces and split
1	cup Marinara Sauce (see recipe on page 204)
2	loaves French bread

In a skillet heat the oil and sauté the onions and peppers until tender. Place the sausages meat side up under the oven broiler long enough to char. Add the sausages to the onions and peppers. Add the marinara sauce and simmer until heated through.

Split open the French bread. Fill with sausage, peppers, and onions.

Note: Due to the high beta carotene content of marinara sauce, drinking tea with this sandwich is recommended.

IRON	*per serving*	
	heme iron MILLIGRAMS	nonheme iron MILLIGRAMS
	0.4	0.7

Sloppy Joes
Serves 6

2	tablespoons olive oil
½	cup finely chopped onion
½	cup finely chopped green bell pepper
¼	cup finely chopped celery
1	pound ground turkey
1	teaspoon salt
½	teaspoon red pepper
1	teaspoon cumin
1	teaspoon minced garlic
3	tablespoons tomato paste
½	cup hot coffee
⅔	cup catsup
8	whole-wheat hamburger buns

IS LOW IN HEME IRON AND CONTAINS

THIS RECIPE	substances that inhibit absorption of nonheme IRON	
	calcium	
	dairy phosphate	
	eggs	
	phytate phosphorus	
	X	polyphenols tannic acid chlorogenic acid phenolic acid
	oxalates	

In a skillet heat the oil and sauté the onion, bell pepper, and celery until tender. Add the turkey, salt, red pepper, cumin, and garlic, and sauté until the turkey is done. Add the tomato paste, hot coffee, and catsup. Simmer for 20 to 30 minutes. Serve on whole-wheat hamburger buns.

IRON	per serving heme iron MILLIGRAMS	nonheme iron MILLIGRAMS
	0.52	0.6

Tuna Bacon Melt
Serves 2

⅔   **cup tuna salad**

2   **slices toasted rye bread**

3   **strips crisp bacon, crumbled**

4   **slices Swiss cheese, cut julienne style**

Divide the tuna salad onto the rye toast. Cover with crumbled bacon and cheese. Place under the broiler to melt the cheese.

IS LOW IN HEME IRON AND CONTAINS	
THIS RECIPE	substances that inhibit absorption of nonheme **IRON**
	X calcium
	X dairy phosphate
	eggs
	X phytate phosphorus
	X polyphenols tannic acid chlorogenic acid phenolic acid
	oxalates

IRON	per serving	
	heme iron MILLIGRAMS	nonheme iron MILLIGRAMS
	0.3	0.7

Tuna Melt with Black Olives and Roasted Peppers

Serves 1

¼   **cup red or green bell pepper strips**
     Olive oil
½   **toasted English muffin**
1   **serving (about ⅓ cup) tuna salad**
2   **tablespoons chopped black olives**
1   **ounce shredded sharp Cheddar cheese**

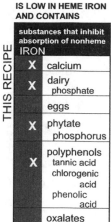

THIS RECIPE	IS LOW IN HEME IRON AND CONTAINS	
	substances that inhibit absorption of nonheme **IRON**	
	X	calcium
	X	dairy phosphate
		eggs
	X	phytate phosphorus
	X	polyphenols tannic acid chlorogenic acid phenolic acid
		oxalates

Brush the pepper with olive oil and cut into slivers. Place on a baking sheet and roast under the broiler until slightly burnt at the edges.

Toast the English muffin half. Scoop tuna onto the muffin. Add black olives and peppers. Cover the top with cheese. Heat under the broiler until the cheese melts or heat in the microwave (take care; bread can get tough).

⁺RON	*per serving* heme iron MILLIGRAMS	nonheme iron MILLIGRAMS
	0.6	0.8

Turkey Club

Serves 4

8	ounces fresh baked turkey breast
8	strips bacon
2	tablespoons mayonnaise
1	tablespoon spicy mustard
12	slices whole-wheat bread
4	slices deli ham
4	lettuce leaves
4	slices tomato

Bake the turkey breast for 1 hour. Wrap and cool in the refrigerator overnight.

In the microwave cook the bacon until crisp.

In a small bowl combine the mayonnaise and mustard.

Toast the bread. Spread 4 slices of toast with the mayonnaise and mustard sauce. Top with ham and 2 slices of bacon. Top each with another slice of toast. Spread with sauce. Layer 2 ounces of sliced turkey, then lettuce and tomato on each sandwich. Top each sandwich with a piece of toast. Slice each club on the diagonal (corner to corner), creating triangles. Secure each triangle with a toothpick.

IRON	per serving	
	heme iron MILLIGRAMS	nonheme iron MILLIGRAMS
	0.5	1.4

Turkey Wrap with Pepper Mayonnaise
Serves 4

½	cup mayonnaise
¼	teaspoon black pepper
4	soft pita pockets
12	ounces thinly sliced turkey breast
4	slices Swiss cheese
4	fresh spinach leaves
4	thin slices red onion

In a small bowl mix the mayonnaise with the black pepper. Spread on the pita pockets. Layer turkey, cheese, spinach, and onion, fold in half, and serve.

THIS RECIPE IS LOW IN HEME IRON AND CONTAINS

substances that inhibit absorption of nonheme IRON

X	calcium
X	dairy phosphate
	eggs
X	phytate phosphorus
X	polyphenols tannic acid chlorogenic acid phenolic acid
X	oxalates

IRON	per serving	
	heme iron MILLIGRAMS	nonheme iron MILLIGRAMS
	trace	0.6

Veggie Pocket
Serves 4

1	cup chopped leaf lettuce
¼	cup chopped onion
¼	cup cucumbers, scored and sliced thin
2	tablespoons Italian dressing
4	pita pockets
½	cup shredded sharp Cheddar cheese

In a medium bowl toss the lettuce, onion, and cucumber with the dressing. Fill pita pockets with salad and add cheese.

THIS RECIPE IS LOW IN HEME IRON AND CONTAINS

substances that inhibit absorption of nonheme IRON

	calcium
X	dairy phosphate
	eggs
X	phytate phosphorus
	polyphenols tannic acid chlorogenic acid phenolic acid
	oxalates

IRON	per serving	
	heme iron MILLIGRAMS	nonheme iron MILLIGRAMS
	0.0	0.6

Welsh Rarebit
Serve 4

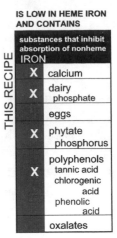

THIS RECIPE	IS LOW IN HEME IRON AND CONTAINS	
	substances that inhibit absorption of nonheme IRON	
	X	calcium
	X	dairy phosphate
		eggs
	X	phytate phosphorus
	X	polyphenols tannic acid chlorogenic acid phenolic acid
		oxalates

¼   cup olive oil
2   tablespoons flour
1½ cups milk
½   cup brewed tea
1   cup cubed Velveeta cheese
1   cup shredded sharp Cheddar cheese
2   tablespoons tomato paste
1   teaspoon Worcestershire sauce
½   pound deli ham, shredded

In a saucepan heat the oil. Whisk the flour into the hot oil. Add the milk and tea, and blend well. Add the Velveeta, and stir until melted. Add the Cheddar, tomato paste, and Worcestershire sauce, and heat through. Then add the meat and reheat.

Serve over toasted rye.

IRON	per serving	
	heme iron MILLIGRAMS	nonheme iron MILLIGRAMS
	0.3	0.8

Barbecued Chicken

Serves 4 (Makes 4½ cups of sauce, serving size: approximately 2 tablespoons)

4	tablespoons olive oil
1	cup finely chopped onion
2	teaspoons minced garlic
1	small can tomato paste
2	cans hot strong black coffee
1	cup Heinz catsup
¼	cup apple cider vinegar
½	cup brown sugar
2	tablespoons spicy mustard
½	teaspoon red pepper

4	7- to 8-ounce chicken breasts on the bone

THIS RECIPE **IS LOW IN HEME IRON AND CONTAINS** substances that inhibit absorption of nonheme **IRON**

	calcium
	dairy phosphate
	eggs
	phytate phosphorus
X X	polyphenols tannic acid chlorogenic acid phenolic acid
	oxalates

In a saucepan heat the oil and sauté the onion and garlic until tender and golden, about 20 minutes.

Add the remaining ingredients except the chicken and simmer for 1 hour.

Refrigerate the sauce and use as needed.

Trim all excess fat from the chicken. Wash the chicken in cold water, pat dry, and place in glass cooking dish. Cover and bake at 350° for 1 hour.

Allow the meat to cool so the skin can be removed without burning fingers. Drain the broth and refrigerate for use in soup, rice, or sauces.

Once the skin is removed, generously cover the meat with barbecue sauce. Place the chicken under the broiler for 5 to 10 minutes until the barbecue sauce begins to char slightly. Remove and let stand for 10 minutes before serving.

IRON	per serving heme iron MILLIGRAMS	nonheme iron MILLIGRAMS
	0.4	0.8

Breaded Eggplant with Marinara Sauce
Serves 4

4	cups Marinara Sauce (see recipe on page 204)
	Pasta (linguini, angel hair, ziti, or your preference)
7	cups water
1	cup brewed tea
1	teaspoon salt
1	cup olive oil
1	medium eggplant with skin
2	cups flour for dredging
2	eggs, lightly beaten
2	cups bread crumbs
1	teaspoon salt
½	cup grated Parmesan cheese

THIS RECIPE IS LOW IN HEME IRON AND CONTAINS

substances that inhibit absorption of nonheme IRON	
X	calcium
X	dairy phosphate
X	eggs
X	phytate phosphorus
X X	polyphenols tannic acid chlorogenic acid phenolic acid
	oxalates

Heat the marinara sauce and have ready to serve.

Prepare the pasta: In a large pot bring the water to a boil with the tea and 1 teaspoon of salt. Add the pasta and cook according to the time specified on the package.

In a skillet heat the olive oil on medium-high for frying. Wash, dry, and cut the eggplant first lengthwise then into medium width slices. Dredge first in flour, then in the eggs, then in bread crumbs. Drop in hot olive oil, brown, turn and brown the other side. Remove from the oil and place on a paper towel to drain. Sprinkle salt lightly over the surface of the fried eggplant.

On warm plates place the eggplant next to a serving of pasta, cover both with marinara, and top with Parmesan cheese.

IRON	per serving heme iron MILLIGRAMS	nonheme iron MILLIGRAMS
	0.0	0.95

Brunch Frittata

Serves 6 to 8

2	tablespoons olive oil
½	cup finely chopped yellow onion
½	teaspoon minced garlic
1	cup sliced mushrooms
½	cup chopped green pepper
½	cup ripe olives
5	eggs
⅓	cup light cream
1	teaspoon salt
⅛	teaspoon white pepper
1	8-ounce package Neufchatel cheese, cut into small pieces
1	cup shredded Swiss cheese
1⅓	cups torn rye bread

THIS RECIPE **IS LOW IN HEME IRON AND CONTAINS** substances that inhibit absorption of nonheme IRON

X	calcium
X	dairy phosphate
X	eggs
X	phytate phosphorus
X X	polyphenols tannic acid chlorogenic acid phenolic acid
	oxalates

In a skillet heat the olive oil and sauté the onion and garlic. Add the mushrooms, green pepper, and olives.

In a medium bowl mix the eggs, cream, salt, white pepper, Neufchatel cheese, and ½ cup of Swiss cheese. Spray a small square glass baking dish with vegetable spray. Line the bottom of the dish with bread. Slowly pour the mixture into the pan; stir to assure all ingredients are evenly distributed. Bake uncovered at 350° for 45 to 50 minutes. Let stand 10 minutes before serving.

IRON	*per serving* heme iron MILLIGRAMS	nonheme iron MILLIGRAMS
	trace	1.2

Buckwheat Pancakes with Spiced Apples and Coffee Syrup (Faux Molasses)

Serves 4 to 6

SPICED APPLES:

2	**cups chopped apples**
¼	**cup apple juice**
1	**teaspoon cinnamon**
2	**cups Faux Molasses (see recipe on page 216)**

BUCKWHEAT PANCAKES:

2	**tablespoons olive oil**
1½	**cups buckwheat flour**
1½	**teaspoons baking powder**
1	**teaspoon baking soda**
1	**teaspoon salt**
1	**teaspoon instant coffee**
1½	**cups buttermilk**
2	**eggs, lightly beaten**
1	**teaspoon vanilla extract**

THIS RECIPE **IS LOW IN HEME IRON AND CONTAINS** substances that inhibit absorption of nonheme IRON

X	calcium
X	dairy phosphate
X	eggs
X	phytate phosphorus
X X	polyphenols tannic acid chlorogenic acid
X	phenolic acid
	oxalates

Place the apples in a saucepan with the apple juice, cinnamon, and 1 cup of Faux Molasses. Simmer until done. Set aside.

In a glass skillet heat the oil to medium-high. Place in a flour sifter all dry ingredients: flour, baking powder, soda, salt, and coffee.

In a medium bowl mix the buttermilk, eggs, and vanilla. Sift the dry ingredients into the egg-milk mixture (*Tip:* put the batter into a large measuring cup with spout for ease in pouring). Pour 4 equal dollops of batter into the hot skillet. Leave ample room as the cakes will expand. When bubbles form in the center of each cake, flip over to brown the other side. Remove and place on a warm plate.

Repeat until all batter is used.`

Serve the pancakes topped with apples and the remaining Faux Molasses.

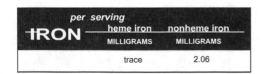

IRON	*per serving*	
	heme iron MILLIGRAMS	nonheme iron MILLIGRAMS
	trace	2.06

Carbonara
Serves 4

7	cups water
1	cup brewed tea
1	teaspoon salt
1	pound angel hair pasta
¼	cup olive oil
⅓	cup each: shredded fontina, havarti, Parmesan cheeses
4	strips crisp bacon, crumbled
1	teaspoon fresh chopped parsley

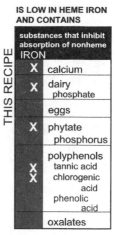

THIS RECIPE	IS LOW IN HEME IRON AND CONTAINS	
	substances that inhibit absorption of nonheme IRON	
	X	calcium
	X	dairy phosphate
		eggs
	X	phytate phosphorus
	X X	polyphenols tannic acid chlorogenic acid phenolic acid
		oxalates

In a stockpot bring the water to a boil with the tea and salt. Add the pasta and cook according to the time specified on the package. Rinse, drain, and return to the warm pot. Toss with olive oil. Add the cheeses, toss, and add bacon and parsley.

IRON	per serving	
	heme iron MILLIGRAMS	nonheme iron MILLIGRAMS
	0.2	2.0

Chicken Asparagus Casserole
Serves 4 to 6

3	to 4 chicken breasts with ribs
2	cups water
1	cup brewed tea
1	cup Chicken Velouté (see recipe on page 201)
1	cup sour cream
¼	cup mayonnaise
1	10-ounce box frozen chopped asparagus
1	cup wild rice
1	cup water
1	cup brewed strong black tea
½	teaspoon salt

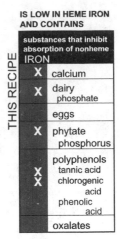

IS LOW IN HEME IRON
AND CONTAINS

THIS RECIPE	substances that inhibit absorption of nonheme IRON	
	X	calcium
	X	dairy phosphate
		eggs
	X	phytate phosphorus
	X X	polyphenols tannic acid chlorogenic acid phenolic acid
	-	
		oxalates

In a stockpot simmer the chicken breasts with rib in 2 cups of water and 1 cup of tea for 45 minutes. Remove the chicken and cool. Use the broth to prepare the velouté while the chicken cools.

Prepare the velouté and add the sour cream and mayonnaise.

Thaw the asparagus but do not cook. Place in a glass baking dish. When the chicken is sufficiently cooled, remove the meat from the bone and tear into pieces. Layer on top of the asparagus. Pour the sauce over the layered chicken and spread evenly. Bake at 375° for 1 hour or until brown.

Meanwhile prepare the rice. In a stockpot bring the water to a boil with the tea and salt. Add the rice, reduce the heat, cover, and steam for 25 minutes.

Serve the casserole over rice.

IRON	*per serving*	
	heme iron MILLIGRAMS	nonheme iron MILLIGRAMS
	0.2	0.5

Chicken Carbonara with Noodles Verte
Serves 4

7	cups water
1	cup brewed tea
1	teaspoon salt
½	pound spinach noodles
4	tablespoons olive oil
3	boneless skinless chicken breasts, cut into strips
¼	cup chopped prosciutto (Italian ham)
1	cup sliced mushrooms
¼	cup dry white wine
4	tablespoons whole-wheat flour
1	teaspoon salt
¼	teaspoon white pepper
½	cup strong coffee
1	cup chicken broth
½	cup light cream
¼	cup grated Parmesan cheese

THIS RECIPE

IS LOW IN HEME IRON AND CONTAINS

	substances that inhibit absorption of nonheme IRON
X	calcium
X	dairy phosphate
X	eggs
X	phytate phosphorus
X X	polyphenols tannic acid chlorogenic acid phenolic acid
X	oxalates

In a large pot bring the water to a boil with the tea and salt. Add the noodles and cook according to the time specified on the package.

In a skillet heat 2 tablespoons of oil and sauté the chicken until brown on the edges. Remove the chicken and set aside. To the drippings add the ham, mushrooms, and wine, and continue cooking until the wine evaporates. Remove the mushroom/ham mixture. Add 2 tablespoons of oil to the pan. Whisk in the flour, salt, and pepper. Slowly add the coffee and whisk until the paste thickens. Add the broth and whisk until the sauce thickens. Add the ham-mushroom mixture, then stir in the light cream. Pour the sauce over the noodles, place the chicken strips on top, and sprinkle with Parmesan cheese.

IRON	per serving	
	heme iron MILLIGRAMS	nonheme iron MILLIGRAMS
	0.5	1.3

Chicken Pot Pie

6 servings

2	chicken breasts, 1 leg, and 1 thigh
2	cups water
1	cup brewed strong black tea
1	teaspoon salt
4	tablespoons olive oil
½	cup finely chopped onion
½	cup finely chopped celery
½	cup sliced mushrooms
4	tablespoons flour
	Pastry for a 2-crust pie (or buttermilk biscuit dough)
½	cup spring peas
½	cup cooked carrots
	Black pepper to taste
½	cup sour cream

IS LOW IN HEME IRON AND CONTAINS

THIS RECIPE	substances that inhibit absorption of nonheme **IRON**	
	X	calcium
	X	dairy phosphate
		eggs
	X	phytate phosphorus
	X X	polyphenols tannic acid chlorogenic acid phenolic acid
		oxalates

In a saucepan simmer the chicken in 2 cups of water with 1 cup of tea for 45 minutes.

Remove the meat from the broth and set aside until cool. When cool enough to touch, pull the chicken from the bone and tear into small pieces—do not cut up the meat. Add 1 tablespoon of salt to the broth; reserve for sauce.

In a stockpot heat 2 tablespoons of olive oil and sauté the onion until tender. Add the celery and cook until tender. Add the mushrooms and cook 10 more minutes.

In a glass saucepan heat 2 tablespoons of the olive oil. Sprinkle the flour into the oil and whisk until a paste forms. Gently pour some of the broth into the paste; whisk until the sauce thickens, then slowly continue to add the broth a bit at a time so the sauce remains thick. Add the onion, celery, and mushrooms.

Line a baking dish with piecrust. Place a layer of pulled chicken on top of the crust. Add the spring peas and carrots. Season with black pepper to taste. Pour 2 cups of sauce over the layers. Reserve the remaining sauce for creamy gravy. Place the remaining crust on top, pinch the edges shut, and pierce the top with a fork to allow hot air to vent. Bake at 400° to 425° until the top crust is brown, about 50 minutes.

Heat the remaining sauce to a gentle boil. Reduce the heat and stir in the sour cream. Sauce can be optional on each serving of pot pie.

IRON	*per serving*	
	heme iron MILLIGRAMS	nonheme iron MILLIGRAMS
	0.25	2.8

Chicken Cordon Bleu
Serves 4

4	boneless chicken breasts (4 ounces each)
½	pound Swiss cheese
4	slices prosciutto (Italian ham)
1	cup flour for dredging
2	eggs, lightly beaten
1	cup whole-wheat bread crumbs
1	cup olive oil

THIS RECIPE IS LOW IN HEME IRON AND CONTAINS

substances that inhibit absorption of nonheme IRON	
X	calcium
X	dairy phosphate
X	eggs
X	phytate phosphorus
X X	polyphenols tannic acid chlorogenic acid phenolic acid
	oxalates

Place the chicken between 2 sheets of waxed paper. Gently pound the chicken until flattened. Place 2 ounces of cheese and 1 slice of ham in the center of each piece of chicken. Fold the flaps to the center, then roll up. Dredge in flour, then in egg, and finally the bread crumbs.

   In a skillet heat the oil. Make certain the oil is very hot. Fry the rolled and breaded chicken until lightly browned. Remove and drain on paper towels. Place seam side down in a shallow baking dish. Cover and bake at 350° for 40 minutes.

IRON	*per serving* heme iron MILLIGRAMS	nonheme iron MILLIGRAMS
	0.5	0.76

Chicken and Herbed Dumplings

Serves 4

2	cups flour
1	teaspoon baking powder
2	teaspoons salt
8	cups hot chicken broth
1	egg, lightly beaten
1	tablespoon fresh chopped parsley
1	teaspoon chives
¼	teaspoon thyme
¼	teaspoon oregano
¼	teaspoon white pepper
1	cup brewed strong black tea
1	cup Chicken Velouté (see recipe on page 201)
½	cup light cream
3	chicken breasts, boiled and meat pulled from bone

THIS RECIPE **IS LOW IN HEME IRON AND CONTAINS** substances that inhibit absorption of nonheme **IRON**

X	calcium
X	dairy phosphate
X	eggs
X	phytate phosphorus
X X	polyphenols tannic acid chlorogenic acid phenolic acid
X	oxalates

In a medium bowl sift together the flour, baking powder, and 1 teaspoon of the salt. Add 1 cup of hot broth, then add the lightly beaten egg (do this quickly or the egg will cook). Fold in the herbs and pepper. Place the dough on a floured pastry cloth and roll out until about ¼ inch thick.

In a stockpot bring the remaining broth, tea, and remaining 1 teaspoon of salt to a boil. Cut the dumplings into 2-inch squares and drop in boiling tea broth. The dumplings will float when done. Remove the dumplings and set aside.

Heat the velouté and add the cream. Stir in the chicken, and serve over the dumplings.

IRON	*per serving*	
	heme iron	nonheme iron
	MILLIGRAMS	MILLIGRAMS
	0.3	0.8

Cubed Steak
Serves 4

4	cubed beef steaks
2	cups brewed tea
4	tablespoons olive oil
	Flour for dredging
	Salt and pepper to taste

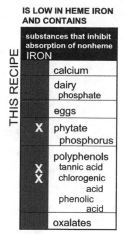

	IS LOW IN HEME IRON AND CONTAINS	
THIS RECIPE	substances that inhibit absorption of nonheme IRON	
		calcium
		dairy phosphate
		eggs
	X	phytate phosphorus
	X X	polyphenols tannic acid chlorogenic acid phenolic acid
		oxalates

Allow the meat to marinate overnight in the tea.

In a skillet heat the olive oil for frying. Dredge the meat in flour. Brown the meat on both sides. Lightly salt and pepper the meat. Lower the heat, cover, and continue cooking for 10 minutes. Cut off the heat but do not lift the lid, and steam the meat for another 40 minutes.

Note: Beef contains high amounts of heme iron. Enjoy this entrée with low iron vegetables such as steamed collard greens, sautéed zucchini, sliced cucumber and onion salad, and tea as a beverage.

IRON	per serving heme iron MILLIGRAMS	nonheme iron MILLIGRAMS
	0.8	1.2

Gumbo with Turkey Sausage
Serves 6

6	cups Gumbo (see recipe on page 203)
1½	pounds turkey sausage
1	cup broth
1	cup brewed tea
1	teaspoon salt
1	cup rice
½	cup chopped spring onions
3	cups cooked black or red beans (see recipe on page 177)

IS LOW IN HEME IRON AND CONTAINS

THIS RECIPE

substances that inhibit absorption of nonheme IRON	
X	calcium
X	dairy phosphate
	eggs
X	phytate phosphorus
X X	polyphenols tannic acid chlorogenic acid phenolic acid
	oxalates

In a saucepan heat the gumbo on medium low. Cut the turkey sausage diagonally into 1-inch pieces; split in half. Place in a baking dish under the broiler until the meat is slightly burned. Remove from the oven and add to the gumbo.

In a large saucepan bring the broth, tea, and salt to a boil. Add the rice. Cover, reduce the heat, and steam for 25 minutes.

Heat the beans in the microwave.

In large bowls place rice, then beans, cover with gumbo and meat. Top with spring onions.

IRON	per serving	
	heme iron MILLIGRAMS	nonheme iron MILLIGRAMS
	0.6	0.67

Ham with Mustard Sauce

Serves 4

1	pound ham steak, thickly sliced
1	cup strong coffee
2	tablespoons olive oil
4	tablespoons whole-wheat flour
6	tablespoons dry mustard
½	cup light cream

In a large skillet over medium-high heat sear the ham. Add ½ cup of coffee and cool until the liquid evaporates. Remove the meat and set aside. Add olive oil to the pan. Whisk in the flour and mustard. When the paste browns, slowly add the remaining coffee. When the mixture thickens, slowly add the cream. Heat through. Serve the sauce over the meat.

IS LOW IN HEME IRON AND CONTAINS

THIS RECIPE	substances that inhibit absorption of nonheme IRON	
	X	calcium
	X	dairy phosphate
		eggs
	X	phytate phosphorus
	X X	polyphenols tannic acid chlorogenic acid phenolic acid
		oxalates

IRON	per serving	
	heme iron MILLIGRAMS	nonheme iron MILLIGRAMS
	0.4	0.6

Herb Encrusted Chicken

Serves 4

	IS LOW IN HEME IRON AND CONTAINS	
THIS RECIPE	substances that inhibit absorption of nonheme IRON	
	X	calcium
	X	dairy phosphate
		eggs
	X	phytate phosphorus
	X X	polyphenols tannic acid chlorogenic acid phenolic acid
		oxalates

4   chicken breasts with ribs, skin removed and fat trimmed
1   cup buttermilk
1   teaspoon each: marjoram, thyme, rosemary, dill, and
       garlic powder
½   teaspoon paprika
½   teaspoon salt
¼   teaspoon red pepper
¼   teaspoon sugar

In a large bowl soak the chicken in buttermilk meat side down.

In a small bowl combine all herbs, seasonings, and sugar. Coat each chicken breast with the herb mixture until all of the mixture is used. Cover and bake at 375° for 45 minutes.

Remove the cover, increase the oven temperature to 400°, and bake an additional 10 minutes.

IRON	*per serving*	
	heme iron MILLIGRAMS	nonheme iron MILLIGRAMS
	0.4	0.6

Italian Chicken

Serves 6

1	whole chicken
4	cups Marinara Sauce (see recipe on page 204)
2	bay leaves
1	tablespoon oregano
1	pound pasta
7	cups water
1	cup brewed tea
1	teaspoon salt
½	cup Parmesan or Romano cheese

THIS RECIPE

IS LOW IN HEME IRON AND CONTAINS

	substances that inhibit absorption of nonheme IRON
X	calcium
X	dairy phosphate
	eggs
X	phytate phosphorus
X X	polyphenols tannic acid chlorogenic acid phenolic acid
X	oxalates

Rinse the chicken in cold water and place in a baking dish. Cover with marinara sauce. Add bay leaves and oregano. Cover and bake at 300° for 2 hours.

Uncover and let stand for 10 minutes. Prepare the pasta in boiling water with tea and salt according to the time specified on the package (angel hair 6 minutes, vermicelli 7, etc.). Rinse, drain, and set aside.

Remove the bay leaves and discard. Separate the chicken from the bones, cartilage, and fat. Return the chicken to the sauce. Dump the pasta into the chicken-marinara sauce, toss, and turn out on warm plates. Top with cheese.

IRON	*per serving* heme iron MILLIGRAMS	nonheme iron MILLIGRAMS
	0.5	1.9

Layered Taco Salad
Serves 6

2	cups cooked black beans
1½	cups shredded Cheddar or Monterey Jack cheese
4	cups shredded iceberg lettuce
1	teaspoon salt
1	cup diced fresh tomatoes
¼	cup sliced pitted black olives
2	roasted, peeled, and chopped poblano peppers
¼	cup chopped green onions
1	cup avocado dip
½	teaspoon cumin
2	cups coarsely crushed tortilla chips

In the bottom of a glass casserole dish layer in order the beans, cheese, lettuce, (sprinkle salt over lettuce layer), tomatoes, olives, peppers, and onions.

In a medium bowl mix together the avocado dip and cumin. Spread the avocado mixture over the top of the layered salad. Cover the dish with film wrap and refrigerate overnight.

Serve the salad over crushed tortilla chips.

THIS RECIPE IS LOW IN HEME IRON AND CONTAINS

substances that inhibit absorption of nonheme IRON

X	calcium
X	dairy phosphate
	eggs
X	phytate phosphorus
X X	polyphenols tannic acid chlorogenic acid phenolic acid
	oxalates

IRON	per serving	
	heme iron MILLIGRAMS	nonheme iron MILLIGRAMS
	trace	2.2

Marinated Chicken

Serves 4

1	cup strong brewed tea
¼	cup balsamic vinegar
1	tablespoon minced garlic
1	teaspoon oregano
4	boneless chicken breasts, skin and fat removed
1	tablespoon cornstarch
¼	teaspoon salt
¼	cup water

IS LOW IN HEME IRON AND CONTAINS

THIS RECIPE	substances that inhibit absorption of nonheme IRON	
		calcium
		dairy phosphate
		eggs
		phytate phosphorus
	X	polyphenols tannic acid chlorogenic acid phenolic acid
	X	oxalates

In a flat glass casserole dish combine the tea, vinegar, garlic, and oregano. Rinse and pat dry each piece of chicken and place in the marinade. Refrigerate overnight, turning the meat once.

Place the chicken under the broiler for 8 minutes per side. Pour the marinade into a skillet.

In a shaker container mix the cornstarch, salt, and water. Shake vigorously and pour into the boiling marinade. Cook until the sauce is the consistency of gravy. Drizzle the sauce over the broiled chicken.

IRON	per serving	
	heme iron MILLIGRAMS	nonheme iron MILLIGRAMS
	0.4	0.6

Marinated Flank Steak

Serves 4

MARINADE:

2	cups hot strong coffee
1/4	cup honey
1	tablespoon ground ginger
1	tablespoon soy sauce

1½   pounds flank steak

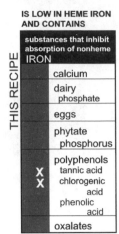

IS LOW IN HEME IRON AND CONTAINS		
	substances that inhibit absorption of nonheme	
THIS RECIPE	IRON	
		calcium
		dairy phosphate
		eggs
		phytate phosphorus
	X X	polyphenols tannic acid chlorogenic acid phenolic acid
		oxalates

In a flat glass casserole dish combine the coffee, honey, ginger, and soy sauce. Place the meat in the dish and marinate in the refrigerator for 24 hours.

Remove the meat from the marinade. Prepare a grill.

Grill the meat on each side for 5 minutes, or place under the broiler for 10 minutes. Let stand for 10 minutes before slicing.

Slice the meat on an angle in thin slices.

Note: Due to the high heme content of this recipe, drink tea and serve this entrée with low-iron vegetables such as ½ cup green beans (0.37) and ½ cup fried cabbage and onions (0.45).

IRON	*per serving*	
	heme iron MILLIGRAMS	nonheme iron MILLIGRAMS
	1.1	3.2

Meatballs and Perciatelli (Long Thin Macaroni)

Makes 24 meatballs; serves 8

IS LOW IN HEME IRON AND CONTAINS	
substances that inhibit absorption of nonheme IRON	
X	calcium
X	dairy phosphate
X	eggs
X	phytate phosphorus
X X	polyphenols tannic acid chlorogenic acid phenolic acid
	oxalates

THIS RECIPE

2	pounds ground turkey
1	teaspoon garlic powder
¼	cup chopped parsley
1	teaspoon salt
1	teaspoon black pepper
1	cup dried bread crumbs
⅔	cup grated Parmesan or Romano cheese
4	eggs
¾	cup buttermilk
8	cups Marinara Sauce (see recipe on page 204)
2	quarts water
1	teaspoon tea
1	teaspoon salt
1	pound perciatelli

Place the meat in a mixing bowl and add the garlic powder, parsley, salt, pepper, bread crumbs, and cheese. Add the eggs and buttermilk. Work the mixture by hand until well blended (sides of the bowl will be clean). Shape the mixture into 24 balls. Place on a lightly oiled cookie sheet and bake at 350° for 10 minutes.

Remove, drain, and place in marinara sauce. Simmer for 30 to 40 minutes.

In a large pot boil the water, tea, and salt. Drop the noodles into boiling water and cook for 15 to 18 minutes. Drain and rinse.

Serve the meatballs and sauce over the perciatelli.

IRON	per serving	
	heme iron MILLIGRAMS	nonheme iron MILLIGRAMS
	0.4	2.1

Meat Loaf

Serves 4

1 egg
½ cup strong black cold coffee
¼ cup oatmeal
¼ cup whole-wheat bread crumbs
1 pound ground turkey
¼ cup finely chopped onion
½ teaspoon salt
¼ teaspoon pepper
⅓ cup catsup

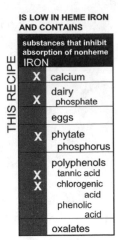

IS LOW IN HEME IRON AND CONTAINS

THIS RECIPE	substances that inhibit absorption of nonheme IRON	
	X	calcium
	X	dairy phosphate
		eggs
	X	phytate phosphorus
	X X	polyphenols tannic acid chlorogenic acid phenolic acid
		oxalates

In a large bowl lightly beat the egg and add the coffee. Add the oatmeal and bread crumbs, and mix well. Add the remaining ingredients except catsup, and combine well (the best way is by hand). Place in a glass loaf pan. Spread catsup over the top. Cover and bake at 350° for 40 minutes.

Uncover and continue baking for 15 minutes. Let the meat loaf stand for 10 to 15 minutes before serving.

Approximate iron per serving: heme 0.4, nonheme 2.3

This recipe is low in heme iron and contains tannins, chlorogenic acid, phytate phosphorus, phosphates, calcium.

IRON	per serving	
	heme iron MILLIGRAMS	nonheme iron MILLIGRAMS
	0.4	2.3

Mixed Grill Stir-Fry

Serves 4

½ cup strong black tea
¼ cup teriyaki sauce
1 teaspoon honey
1 tablespoon ground ginger
⅓ pound raw shrimp, cleaned
⅓ pound sirloin steak strips
⅓ pound chicken breast strips
2 cups broth
1 teaspoon salt
1 cup rice
2 tablespoons cornstarch
1 tablespoon olive oil
1 pound fresh asparagus spears, ends snapped
1 yellow summer squash, cut into julienne strips
1 teaspoon fresh chives

THIS RECIPE	IS LOW IN HEME IRON AND CONTAINS	
	substances that inhibit absorption of nonheme IRON	
	X	calcium
	X	dairy phosphate
		eggs
	X	phytate phosphorus
	X X	polyphenols tannic acid chlorogenic acid phenolic acid
		oxalates

In a shallow dish combine the tea, teriyaki, honey, and ginger. Add the shrimp, steak strips, and chicken strips, and marinate overnight in the refrigerator.

Prepare the rice. In a stockpot bring 2 cups of broth, 1 teaspoon of salt, and the rice to a boil. Cook according to the time specified on the rice package.

Reserve ¼ cup of the marinade. In a glass skillet bring the remaining marinade to a boil. Place the reserved ¼ cup of marinade and the cornstarch in a small container with a lid and shake vigorously. Slowly pour the cornstarch-marinade mixture into the boiling liquid. Whisk vigorously until the liquid thickens; set aside.

In a separate skillet heat the olive oil. Sear the meat in the oil until done, about 8 to 10 minutes. Do not overcook; shrimp can get tough and chewy. Transfer the meat to the teriyaki marinade sauce.

Steam the asparagus and squash on the stovetop or in the microwave. Sprinkle the vegetables with chopped fresh chives and serve with the meat.

IRON	per serving	
	heme iron MILLIGRAMS	nonheme iron MILLIGRAMS
	0.6	1.2

Mushroom-Stuffed Pork Chops

Serves 4

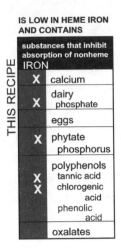

IS LOW IN HEME IRON
AND CONTAINS

THIS RECIPE	substances that inhibit absorption of nonheme IRON	
	X	calcium
	X	dairy phosphate
		eggs
	X	phytate phosphorus
	X X	polyphenols tannic acid chlorogenic acid phenolic acid
		oxalates

4   6-ounce pork chops with pockets (butcher will cut pocket upon request)

1   cup strong black tea

½   cup dry white wine

3   tablespoons olive oil

     Flour for dredging

½   cup finely chopped onion

⅛   teaspoon thyme

1   teaspoon oregano

½   teaspoon black pepper

2   cups sliced mushrooms

½   cup light cream

Trim all visible fat from the chops. In a shallow dish combine the strong tea and white wine and marinate the pork chops overnight in the mixture.

In a glass skillet heat 2 tablespoons of the oil. Dredge the chops in flour and brown in the oil. Remove, drain, and set aside. Add the remaining 1 tablespoon of oil and sauté the onion. Add the thyme, oregano, and pepper, and cook until the onion is tender, about 10 minutes.

Add the mushrooms and ½ cup of the marinade. Cook down until the liquid has evaporated. Spoon the mushroom-herb mixture into the pocket. Retain the pan drippings. Place the pork chops in a glass baking dish, cover, and bake at 300° for 50 minutes. Add the drippings from the baking dish to the previous reserve of drippings in the skillet. Turn up the heat and whisk in 1 teaspoon of flour, then slowly add the remaining marinade. When thickened add the light cream, and heat through. Pour over the chops.

IRON	*per serving*	
	heme iron MILLIGRAMS	nonheme iron MILLIGRAMS
	0.4	0.65

Oven Enchiladas

Serves 8 to 8

2	tablespoons olive oil
½	cup chopped onion
1	pound ground turkey
1	teaspoon cumin
1	teaspoon salt
¼	teaspoon black pepper
4	ounces cream cheese
8	corn tortillas
½	cup enchilada sauce
½	cup shredded Monterey Jack cheese
½	cup sliced black olives
	Jalapeño peppers (optional)

In a large skillet heat the olive oil and sauté the onion until tender. Add the meat and brown. Add the cumin, salt, and pepper. Add the cream cheese and stir until melted.

Wrap the tortillas in foil and warm in a preheated 300° oven.

Spoon the meat-cheese filling onto one end of each tortilla and roll up. Place seam side down in a shallow baking dish. Top with enchilada sauce, shredded Monterey Jack cheese, black olives, and jalapeño peppers. Cover and bake at 350° for 30 to 40 minutes.

IRON	per serving	
	heme iron MILLIGRAMS	nonheme iron MILLIGRAMS
	0.7	3.8

Oven-Fried Catfish

Serves 4

4	catfish fillets
1	cup seedless rye bread crumbs
1	tablespoon whole-wheat flour
1	tablespoon chopped fresh parsley
¼	teaspoon paprika
	Pinch red pepper
2	tablespoons grated Parmesan cheese
1	cup buttermilk
	Nonstick vegetable spray

THIS RECIPE IS LOW IN HEME IRON AND CONTAINS

	substances that inhibit absorption of nonheme IRON
X	calcium
X	dairy phosphate
	eggs
X	phytate phosphorus
X X	polyphenols tannic acid chlorogenic acid phenolic acid
	oxalates

In a shallow dish combine the bread crumbs, flour, parsley, paprika, red pepper, and Parmesan cheese. Coat the fish with buttermilk, then dredge in bread crumb mixture.

Spray a glass baking dish with cooking spray. Place the catfish in the dish. Bake uncovered at 400° for about 20 minutes. Do not overcook; when the fish is done it will be flaky.

IRON	*per serving* heme iron MILLIGRAMS	nonheme iron MILLIGRAMS
	0.3	1.4

Oven-Fried Chicken

Serves 4

½	cup buttermilk
½	cup plain yogurt
4	chicken breasts with ribs, skin and visible fat removed
2	cups bread crumbs
1	teaspoon paprika
1	teaspoon onion powder
1	teaspoon garlic powder
1	teaspoon salt
½	teaspoon oregano
½	teaspoon basil
½	teaspoon pepper

IS LOW IN HEME IRON AND CONTAINS

THIS RECIPE	substances that inhibit absorption of nonheme IRON	
	X	calcium
	X	dairy phosphate
		eggs
	X	phytate phosphorus
	X X	polyphenols tannic acid chlorogenic acid phenolic acid
		oxalates

In a shallow dish mix the buttermilk and yogurt together. Place the chicken meat side down in the mixture and soak for 1 hour.

In a separate shallow dish combine the bread crumbs and remaining ingredients. Coat the chicken in the bread crumb mixture.

Preheat the oven to 400°. Place the chicken meat side up on an ungreased baking sheet. Bake for 45 minutes.

Let the chicken stand for 10 to 15 minutes before serving.

IRON	per serving	
	heme iron MILLIGRAMS	nonheme iron MILLIGRAMS
	0.4	0.6

Parsnips and Pork Roast
Serves 6 to 8

3	to 4 pounds pork roast, all fat trimmed
1	teaspoon rubbed sage
	Oat blend flour for dredging
2	tablespoons olive oil
1	cup strong coffee
	Salt to taste
1	bay leaf
1	teaspoon marjoram
½	pound parsnips, rinsed, ends trimmed

IS LOW IN HEME IRON AND CONTAINS

THIS RECIPE		substances that inhibit absorption of nonheme IRON
		calcium
	X	dairy phosphate
		eggs
	X	phytate phosphorus
	X	polyphenols tannic acid chlorogenic acid phenolic acid
	X	oxalates

Rub the outside of the pork with sage and dredge in flour. In a skillet heat the oil and brown the roast. Place the roast in a large glass casserole with lid. Add the coffee, salt, bay leaf, and marjoram. Cover the roast and bake at 350° for 2½ hours.

Place parsnips around the roast and continue cooking for 15 minutes. Turn the oven off and let the roast and parsnips steam in the oven for 40 minutes. Remove the bay leaf before serving.

Note: Due to the heme iron content of this entrée, serve with other low-iron vegetables and drink tea with this meal.

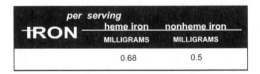

IRON	per serving	
	heme iron MILLIGRAMS	nonheme iron MILLIGRAMS
	0.68	0.5

Pasta e Fagioli (Macaroni and Bean Soup)
Serves 8

1	pound dried navy beans or other small white beans
4	quarts water
3	teaspoons salt
1	teaspoon instant tea
¼	cup olive oil
2	tablespoon minced garlic
1½	cups diced tomatoes
1	cup chicken broth
2	tablespoons chopped fresh parsley
1	teaspoon dried basil
1	pound elbow macaroni
1	cup brewed tea
½	cup Parmesan cheese
½	teaspoon freshly ground black pepper
	Black pepper to taste

THIS RECIPE IS LOW IN HEME IRON AND CONTAINS

substances that inhibit absorption of nonheme IRON	
X	calcium
X	dairy phosphate
	eggs
X	phytate phosphorus
X X	polyphenols tannic acid chlorogenic acid phenolic acid
	oxalates

Wash beans thoroughly, picking out rocks and dirt. In a large pot bring 2 quarts of water to a boil. Add the beans, 1 teaspoon of salt, and tea. Reduce the heat and simmer for 2 hours or until the beans are tender. Drain the beans and set aside.

In a separate stockpot heat the oil and sauté the garlic. Add the tomatoes, chicken broth, 1 teaspoon of salt, parsley, and basil, and simmer at least 20 to 30 minutes.

In a separate pot bring 2 quarts of water to a boil. Add the macaroni, 1 teaspoon of salt, and tea, and cook for 10 minutes. Drain and reserve some of the liquid.

Add the beans and macaroni to the tomato mixture. Adjust the consistency by mashing beans if the dish is too moist, or by adding beans or macaroni broth if too dry. Consistency should be thick (stew-like). Add Parmesan and black pepper.

IRON	per serving	
	heme iron MILLIGRAMS	nonheme iron MILLIGRAMS
	0.0	4.2

Pepper Caraway Chicken
Serves 4

4	**chicken breasts, skin and fat removed**
1	**cup buttermilk**
½	**cup rye bread crumbs with caraway**
½	**teaspoon salt**
¼	**cup coarse ground black pepper**
2	**tablespoons olive oil**

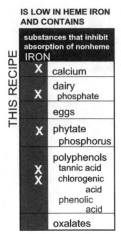

IS LOW IN HEME IRON AND CONTAINS

THIS RECIPE	substances that inhibit absorption of nonheme IRON	
	X	calcium
	X	dairy phosphate
		eggs
	X	phytate phosphorus
	X X	polyphenols tannic acid chlorogenic acid phenolic acid
		oxalates

Rinse the chicken in cold water and pat dry. Place in buttermilk meat side down.

In a shallow dish mix the bread crumbs, salt, and pepper. Dredge the chicken in the crumb mixture, making certain each piece of meat is well coated and the pepper is evenly distributed.

In a skillet heat the oil over medium-high heat. Place the chicken meat side down in the hot oil, reduce the heat to medium, and brown the meat for about 15 to 20 minutes.

Cover the chicken, cut off the heat, and let slow cook for 40 to 45 minutes.

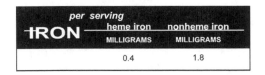

IRON	*per serving*	
	heme iron MILLIGRAMS	nonheme iron MILLIGRAMS
	0.4	1.8

Pork Chops with Barbecued Peppers and Onions

Serves 4

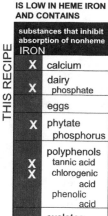

IS LOW IN HEME IRON AND CONTAINS

THIS RECIPE	substances that inhibit absorption of nonheme IRON	
	X	calcium
	X	dairy phosphate
		eggs
	X	phytate phosphorus
	X X	polyphenols tannic acid chlorogenic acid phenolic acid
		oxalates

3 tablespoons olive oil
4 medium-thick center cut pork chops
1 cup flour for dredging
½ cup barbecue sauce
1 cup green pepper strips (julienne style)
1 cup finely chopped onion

In a glass skillet heat 2 tablespoons of olive oil. Lightly coat the chops in flour. Brown the meat on one side, then the other. Remove and place in a shallow baking dish. Cover and bake at 350° for 1 hour.

In a saucepan heat the barbecue sauce.

In a clean skillet heat the remaining tablespoon of oil and sauté the onion and green pepper. Stir the barbecue sauce into the pepper and onion. Serve the sauce over the meat.

IRON	per serving	
	heme iron MILLIGRAMS	nonheme iron MILLIGRAMS
	0.4	1.4

Pork Marsala

Serves 6

1	pound pork tenderloin, sliced into ¼-inch-thick pieces
¼	cup flour
¼	cup olive oil
¼	cup dry white wine
1	cup sliced mushrooms
2	teaspoons salt
¼	cup apple juice
7	cups water
1	cup brewed strong black tea
1	teaspoon salt
12	ounces spinach noodles

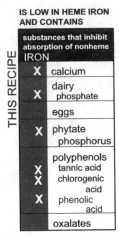

THIS RECIPE IS LOW IN HEME IRON AND CONTAINS

substances that inhibit absorption of nonheme IRON

X	calcium
X	dairy phosphate
	eggs
X	phytate phosphorus
X X	polyphenols tannic acid chlorogenic acid
X	phenolic acid
	oxalates

Dredge the meat in flour. In a skillet heat the oil and brown the tenderloin slices. Set aside.

Add the apple juice to the drippings. Add the mushrooms and cook until the liquid evaporates. Add 1 teaspoon of salt and the wine. Replace the meat, cover, and simmer on very low heat for 30 minutes.

In a stockpot bring the water to a boil with the tea and salt, and drop in the noodles. Boil for 7 to 8 minutes or according to the time specified on the package. Drain and rinse; if necessary reheat in the microwave or oven.

Serve the meat and mushrooms over the noodles.

Note: The alcohol content is lost during cooking.

IRON	per serving heme iron MILLIGRAMS	nonheme iron MILLIGRAMS
	0.4	1.9

Pork Tetrazzini

Serves 6

1	pound lean pork, cut into strips
	Flour for dredging
4	tablespoons olive oil
4	tablespoons flour
1	teaspoon salt
¼	teaspoon white pepper
½	cup dry white wine
1	cup chicken broth
1	cup brewed tea
⅛	teaspoon ground thyme
7	cups water
1	cup brewed tea
1	teaspoon salt
½	pound spaghetti
½	cup grated Parmesan cheese

THIS RECIPE	IS LOW IN HEME IRON AND CONTAINS
	substances that inhibit absorption of nonheme IRON
	calcium
X	dairy phosphate
	eggs
X	phytate phosphorus
X X	polyphenols tannic acid chlorogenic acid phenolic acid
	oxalates

Dredge the pork strips in flour. In a skillet heat 2 tablespoons of olive oil and brown the meat. Set aside.

To the pan drippings add the remaining 2 tablespoons of oil. Whisk in the flour, thyme, salt, and pepper until smooth. Add the wine. Slowly add the broth and 1 cup of tea and whisk until thickened.

In a stockpot bring the water to a boil and add 1 cup of tea and the salt. Add the spaghetti and boil for the length of time suggested on the package. Drain, rinse, and pour into a casserole dish sprayed with vegetable spray. Layer the meat over the spaghetti and cover with sauce. Top with Parmesan cheese. Bake at 350° for 45 minutes.

IRON	per serving	
	heme iron MILLIGRAMS	nonheme iron MILLIGRAMS
	0.5	2.1

Roasted Chicken with Vegetables and Rice

Serves 4

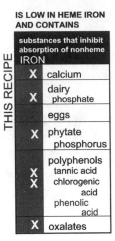

IS LOW IN HEME IRON AND CONTAINS

THIS RECIPE	substances that inhibit absorption of nonheme IRON	
	X	calcium
	X	dairy phosphate
		eggs
	X	phytate phosphorus
	X	polyphenols tannic acid
	X	chlorogenic acid
		phenolic acid
	X	oxalates

1	cup water
1	cup brewed tea
1	teaspoon salt
1	cup basmati rice
½	cup chopped fresh spinach
½	cup diced fresh tomatoes
	Red pepper to taste
1	small whole chicken, excluding organ meats
1	teaspoon salt

In a deep casserole dish place 1 cup of water and the tea. Add the salt, rice, spinach, tomatoes, and red pepper.

Rinse the chicken completely in cold water. Place the chicken in the casserole dish over the rice mixture. Cover and bake at 400° for 30 minutes.

Reduce the heat to 300° and continue cooking for 1 hour.

Remove the dish from the oven, uncover, and let stand for 10 to 15 minutes.

IRON	*per serving*	
	heme iron MILLIGRAMS	nonheme iron MILLIGRAMS
	0.6	1.9

Salmon Patties with Horseradish Sauce

Serves 6

HORSERADISH SAUCE:

1½	cups sour cream
2	tablespoons horseradish
1	teaspoon lemon juice
6	dashes red pepper sauce
	Salt to taste

SALMON PATTIES:

1	10-ounce can salmon, drained (bones optional)
1	egg
2	tablespoons chopped fresh parsley
	Pinch red pepper
1	cup ground saltine crackers
½	cup olive oil for frying

	IS LOW IN HEME IRON AND CONTAINS
THIS RECIPE	**substances that inhibit absorption of nonheme IRON**
	X calcium
	X dairy phosphate
	X eggs
	X phytate phosphorus
	polyphenols tannic acid chlorogenic acid phenolic acid
	oxalates

In a small bowl combine all of the Horseradish Sauce ingredients and mix well.

In a medium bowl combine the salmon, egg, parsley, red pepper, and ½ cup of cracker crumbs. Form into patties and press into the remaining crumbs.

In a skillet heat the oil and fry the salmon patties until golden brown and crisp. Turn over and fry the other side until crisp. Remove and drain. Serve hot with Horseradish Sauce on the side.

IRON	*per serving*	
	heme iron MILLIGRAMS	nonheme iron MILLIGRAMS
	0.4	1.1

Sausage and Three-Cheese Breakfast Casserole

Serves 6

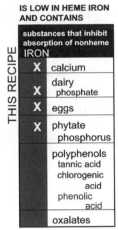

		IS LOW IN HEME IRON AND CONTAINS
THIS RECIPE		**substances that inhibit absorption of nonheme** IRON
	X	calcium
	X	dairy phosphate
	X	eggs
	X	phytate phosphorus
		polyphenols tannic acid chlorogenic acid phenolic acid
		oxalates

4   slices rye bread with caraway seed
4   eggs, lightly beaten
1   cup 1% milk
2   tablespoons olive oil
¼   cup finely chopped onion
1   teaspoon chopped fresh parsley
1   pound turkey sausage
½   cup sliced mushrooms
½   teaspoon salt
    Pinch red pepper
½   cup shredded Vermont or New York sharp white Cheddar
½   cup cubed Swiss cheese
½   cup fontina cheese

Arrange the slices of bread in the bottom of a shallow glass baking dish.

In a medium bowl mix the eggs and milk together and pour over the bread. Cover and refrigerate overnight.

In a skillet heat the olive oil and sauté the onion until tender. Add the parsley, then the sausage, and cook until the meat is done. Add the mushrooms, salt, and red pepper, and cook until the liquid has evaporated.

Layer the meat mixture over the soaked bread and cover with cheeses. Bake uncovered at 350° for 40 minutes.

Let stand for 10 minutes before serving.

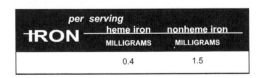

IRON	per serving	
	heme iron MILLIGRAMS	nonheme iron MILLIGRAMS
	0.4	1.5

Seafood Casserole
Serves 6

¼	cup olive oil
2	tablespoons whole-wheat flour
1	teaspoon salt
¼	teaspoon white pepper
½	cup low fat milk
½	teaspoon Worcestershire sauce
¼	cup dry white wine
1	cup grated Swiss cheese
½	cup light cream
1	cup crushed saltine crackers
⅔	pound fresh flounder fillets
⅓	pound small shrimp, cleaned and deveined
1	tablespoon chives

IS LOW IN HEME IRON AND CONTAINS

THIS RECIPE

substances that inhibit absorption of nonheme IRON	
X	calcium
X	dairy phosphate
	eggs
X	phytate phosphorus
	polyphenols tannic acid chlorogenic acid phenolic acid
	oxalates

In a saucepan heat the olive oil. Whisk in the flour, salt, and pepper. Slowly pour in the milk, whisk, and allow to thicken. Add the Worcestershire sauce and wine, and blend well. Add ⅔ cup of Swiss cheese and stir until melted. Drizzle in the cream and heat through, but do not boil.

Spray a glass casserole dish with vegetable spray. Spread crackers over the bottom of the dish. Arrange the fillets on top of the crackers. Spread shrimp evenly over the fillets. Cover the fish with sauce, sprinkle with chives, and top with the remaining cheese. Bake uncovered at 350° for 45 minutes.

IRON	*per serving* heme iron MILLIGRAMS	nonheme iron MILLIGRAMS
	0.2	1.96

Seafood Chowder
Serves 6

1	quart water
1	tablespoon instant tea
¼	pound shelled and deveined shrimp
2	tablespoons olive oil
½	cup finely chopped onion
1	28-ounce can diced tomatoes
3	cups broth
2	tablespoons chopped fresh chives
2	bay leaves
¼	teaspoon thyme
1	tablespoon salt
1	teaspoon coarse black pepper
4	red-skinned potatoes, scrubbed and quartered
½	cup instant potatoes
½	pound haddock fillets cut into large pieces
1	pint light cream

IS LOW IN HEME IRON
AND CONTAINS

THIS RECIPE

	substances that inhibit absorption of nonheme IRON
X	calcium
X	dairy phosphate
	eggs
X	phytate phosphorus
X X	polyphenols tannic acid chlorogenic acid phenolic acid
	oxalates

In a stockpot boil 1 quart of water plus 1 tablespoon of instant tea. Drop in the shrimp, and cook about 5 minutes. The shrimp will curl when done; if overcooked, shrimp are tough.

Remove the shrimp, set aside, and reserve the broth.

In a skillet heat the olive oil and sauté the onion for about 15 minutes. Add the tomatoes and simmer another 15 minutes.

Add the broth, seasonings, and potatoes, and simmer 30 minutes.

Add the instant potatoes, then the haddock, and simmer 20 minutes.

Add the cream and cooked shrimp, and heat but do not boil.

IRON	*per serving*	
	heme iron MILLIGRAMS	nonheme iron MILLIGRAMS
	0.6	2.1

Seafood Lasagna
Serves 6

3	quarts water
1	tablespoon instant tea
1	teaspoon salt
1	pound lasagna
1	cup ricotta cheese
½	cup finely chopped cooked fresh spinach
1	egg
	Leftover fish/shrimp from seafood stock
1	cup mozzarella cheese
½	cup grated Parmesan cheese

EASY ALFREDO SAUCE:

1½	cups sour cream
½	cup grated Parmesan cheese

THIS RECIPE IS LOW IN HEME IRON AND CONTAINS substances that inhibit absorption of nonheme **IRON**

	calcium
X	dairy phosphate
	eggs
	phytate phosphorus
X	polyphenols tannic acid chlorogenic acid phenolic acid
X	oxalates

In a stockpot boil the water, salt, and tea. Drop the lasagna noodles into the boiling water, set a timer, and boil for 6 minutes. Drain, rinse, and set aside the noodles.

In a mixing bowl combine the ricotta, spinach, egg, and fish. Alternate layers of spinach mixture, then mozzarella and Parmesan, ending with cheese. Bake uncovered at 350° for 45 minutes to 1 hour.

Let stand for 15 minutes before serving.

In a small bowl combine the sour cream and Parmesan cheese. Serve the Easy Alfredo Sauce over the top of the lasagna.

IRON	*per serving* heme iron MILLIGRAMS	nonheme iron MILLIGRAMS
	0.4	2.8

Sesame Chicken

Serves 6

1	cup buttermilk
½	cup apple juice
2	cloves garlic, peeled and smashed
4	tablespoons Greek seasoning
1	pound boneless, skinless chicken breasts
2	cups bread crumbs
½	cup sesame seeds
1	6-ounce jar plum jam
1	tablespoon fresh horseradish
1	teaspoon spicy mustard
1	tablespoon apple juice

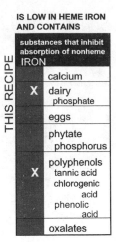

In a shallow dish combine the buttermilk, apple juice, garlic, and Greek seasonings. Soak the chicken in the mixture overnight.

Remove the chicken and dredge in bread crumbs, then sesame seeds. Spray a cookie sheet with vegetable spray. Bake at 400° for about 20 minutes or until golden brown.

In a saucepan combine the plum jam, horseradish, mustard, and apple juice, mix well, and heat through.

Serve the chicken with the mustard plum sauce.

Note: Drinking coffee or tea with this meal is recommended.

IRON	per serving	
	heme iron MILLIGRAMS	nonheme iron MILLIGRAMS
	0.4	3.7

Shrimp Creole

Serves 6

IS LOW IN HEME IRON
AND CONTAINS

THIS RECIPE	substances that inhibit absorption of nonheme IRON	
	calcium	
	dairy	phosphate
	eggs	
	phytate	phosphorus
X	polyphenols	tannic acid chlorogenic acid phenolic acid
	oxalates	

2   tablespoons olive oil

1   cup finely chopped onion

2   stalks celery, strings removed and cut in ½-inch pieces

1   green pepper, seeded and sliced in strips

1   28-ounce can crushed tomatoes with sauce

1   6-ounce can tomato paste

3   cans hot brewed tea (2¼ cups)

1   teaspoon dried basil

1   teaspoon dried thyme

¼   to ½ teaspoon red pepper (depends on personal taste for spiciness)

1   pound shrimp, peeled and deveined (pat dry between paper towels)

2½   cups cooked wild rice

In a stockpot heat the oil and sauté the onions for 15 to 20 minutes until tender. Add the celery and green pepper, and simmer for 5 to 7 minutes.

Add the tomatoes, paste, and hot tea, and mix well. Add the basil, thyme, and pepper. Add the raw shrimp. Bring to a boil and cook until the shrimp curl.

Serve the shrimp and sauce over rice.

Note: Drinking coffee or tea with this meal is recommended.

IRON	per serving	
	heme iron MILLIGRAMS	nonheme iron MILLIGRAMS
	0.5	4.56

Spaghetti with Meat Sauce
Serves 4

½	**pound ground turkey**
¼	**cup coffee**
8	**cups Marinara Sauce (see recipe on page 204)**
2	**quarts water**
1	**teaspoon salt**
1	**teaspoon instant tea**
1	**pound spaghetti of choice**
	Parmesan cheese for topping

THIS RECIPE	IS LOW IN HEME IRON AND CONTAINS		
	substances that inhibit absorption of nonheme		
	IRON		
		calcium	
		dairy phosphate	
		eggs	
		phytate phosphorus	
	X	polyphenols tannic acid chlorogenic acid phenolic acid	
		oxalates	

In a saucepan cook the turkey in the coffee until done. Add the marinara sauce and simmer for 20 to 30 minutes.

In a stockpot bring the water, salt, and tea to a boil. Drop the pasta into the boiling water and stir well. When done, drain and rinse the pasta.

Top with sauce and warm in the microwave.

Sprinkle Parmesan cheese over the sauce.

IRON	per serving	
	heme iron MILLIGRAMS	nonheme iron MILLIGRAMS
	0.3	3.2

Spinach Lasagna
Serves 6

1	cup cooked fresh spinach, drained
24	lasagna noodles
2	eggs
1	cup ricotta cheese
4	cups Marinara Sauce (see recipe on page 204)
2	cups mozzarella cheese
½	cup Parmesan cheese

IS LOW IN HEME IRON AND CONTAINS

THIS RECIPE	substances that inhibit absorption of nonheme IRON	
		calcium
	X	dairy phosphate
		eggs
		phytate phosphorus
	X	polyphenols tannic acid chlorogenic acid phenolic acid
	X	oxalates

Squeeze the excess water out of the spinach by pressing with an absorbent paper towel. Set aside.

Cook the lasagna according to the package directions. Drain and rinse with cool water.

In a medium bowl mix the eggs, ricotta, and spinach together.

In a shallow glass casserole dish begin to layer the lasagna noodles, then spinach mixture, marinara sauce, mozzarella cheese, and Parmesan cheese. Continue to layer, ending with lasagna, reserving some marinara, mozzarella, and Parmesan. Spread a thin layer of marinara sauce over the noodles. Top with mozzarella and parmesan. Bake uncovered at 350° for 45 minutes to 1 hour.

Let stand 15 minutes before serving

IRON	per serving heme iron MILLIGRAMS	nonheme iron MILLIGRAMS
	trace	4.5

Stuffed Chicken Breasts

Serves 4

4	boneless, skinless chicken breasts
1	cup strong tea
1	cup garlic-seasoned croutons
1	3-ounce package Neufchatel cheese
¼	cup Parmesan cheese
¼	teaspoon ground thyme
¼	teaspoon ground rosemary
¼	teaspoon ground basil
¼	teaspoon ground oregano
¼	cup buttermilk
¼	cup crisp crumbled bacon or bacon substitute

THIS RECIPE IS LOW IN HEME IRON AND CONTAINS substances that inhibit absorption of nonheme IRON: calcium; dairy phosphate; eggs; phytate phosphorus; **X** polyphenols tannic acid chlorogenic acid phenolic acid; **X** oxalates

Rinse the chicken in cold water. Marinate overnight in tea.

Drain the chicken and pat dry. Place between sheets of waxed paper and pound with a meat mallet until flattened.

In a food processor grind up the croutons. In a medium bowl mix the cheeses, herbs, and crumbled bacon. Spread one-fourth of the mixture in the center of each piece of chicken and roll the chicken until closed. Dip in the buttermilk, then dredge in the seasoned crumbs. Place seam side down in a casserole dish. Cover and bake at 325° for 1 hour.

IRON	per serving heme iron MILLIGRAMS	nonheme iron MILLIGRAMS
	0.4	1.5

Stuffed Eggplant

Serves 4

1	medium eggplant
1	teaspoon salt
¼	cup crumbled blue cheese
¼	cup Parmesan cheese
¼	cup bread crumbs
1	egg
1	tablespoon flour
½	teaspoon oregano
½	teaspoon basil
½	teaspoon thyme
1	6-ounce can tomato paste
3	cans hot coffee (2¼ cups)
1	teaspoon minced garlic
⅛	teaspoon black pepper
¾	cup grated Swiss cheese

THIS RECIPE IS LOW IN HEME IRON AND CONTAINS substances that inhibit absorption of nonheme **IRON**

	calcium
X	dairy phosphate
X	eggs
	phytate phosphorus
X	polyphenols tannic acid chlorogenic acid phenolic acid
X	oxalates

Wash, dry, and split the eggplant lengthwise. Place in a shallow glass baking dish flesh side down. Add a small amount of water to the dish. Bake at 350° for 30 minutes.

Remove the eggplant. Scoop out the pulp and place in a mixing bowl. Add the remaining ingredients except the Swiss cheese. Pack the mixture into eggplant shells and top with the Swiss cheese. Bake uncovered at 350° for 40 minutes or until the top is golden brown.

Let stand 10 to 15 minutes before serving. Slice across the eggplant for each serving.

†RON	per serving heme iron MILLIGRAMS	nonheme iron MILLIGRAMS
	0.4	1.3

Stuffed Shells with Three Fillings
Serves 6

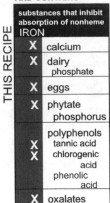

CHEESE FILLING:

½   cup Ricotta cheese

½   cup shredded fontina cheese

½   cup shredded mozzarella cheese

1   egg

¼   teaspoon salt

¼   teaspoon white pepper

TOFU FILLING:

8   ounces tofu, drained

1   egg

¼   cup chopped green pepper

¼   cup chopped mushrooms

¼   cup finely chopped onion

2   tablespoons olive oil

1   teaspoon basil

1   teaspoon fresh parsley

¼   teaspoon salt

¼   teaspoon white pepper

1   teaspoon garlic powder

MEAT FILLING:

½   pound ground veal

¼   cup seedless rye bread crumbs

1   egg

¼   teaspoon salt

¼   teaspoon red pepper

1   teaspoon garlic powder

1   teaspoon basil

1   teaspoon fresh parsley

12   jumbo pasta shells

2   cups Marinara Sauce (see recipe on page 204)

THIS RECIPE

IS LOW IN HEME IRON AND CONTAINS

	substances that inhibit absorption of nonheme IRON
X	calcium
X	dairy phosphate
X	eggs
X	phytate phosphorus
X X	polyphenols tannic acid chlorogenic acid phenolic acid
X	oxalates

In a medium bowl combine all of the ingredients for the desired filling.

Cook the pasta according to the package directions. Drain. Rinse with cold water, drain, and set aside.

Stuff each cooked pasta shell with 2 tablespoons of the filling. Pour a small amount of sauce in the bottom of a glass baking dish. Place the stuffed shells in the sauce and cover with the remaining sauce. Cover and bake at 350° for 40 minutes.

Uncover, turn off the oven, and let stand another 15 minutes in the oven.

Cheese Filling:

IRON	per serving	
	heme iron	nonheme iron
	MILLIGRAMS	MILLIGRAMS
	trace	0.78

Tofu Filling:

IRON	per serving	
	heme iron	nonheme iron
	MILLIGRAMS	MILLIGRAMS
	trace	0.9

Meat Filling:

IRON	per serving	
	heme iron	nonheme iron
	MILLIGRAMS	MILLIGRAMS
	trace	0.9

Sweet-and-Sour Pork

Serves 6

½	cup oil
1	pound lean pork, trimmed and cut into thick strips
½	cup flour
¼	cup brewed strong coffee
1	cup broth
1	cup brewed strong black tea
½	teaspoon salt
1	cup wild rice
1	tablespoon olive oil
1	cup green pepper, cut in julienne strips
½	cup pineapple juice
1	cup soy sauce
½	cup brown sugar
1	tablespoon instant coffee
2	teaspoons cornstarch
¼	cup water

THIS RECIPE IS LOW IN HEME IRON AND CONTAINS

substances that inhibit absorption of nonheme IRON	
X	calcium
X	dairy phosphate
	eggs
X	phytate phosphorus
X X	polyphenols tannic acid chlorogenic acid phenolic acid
	oxalates

In a skillet heat the oil. Dredge the meat in flour and brown in the hot oil. Add the brewed coffee, cover, and reduce the heat. Continue slow cooking the meat for about 45 minutes.

Prepare the rice. In a stockpot bring the broth, tea, and salt to a boil. Add the rice. Cover, reduce the heat, and steam for 25 minutes.

When the meat is done, remove and set aside. Add 1 tablespoon of olive oil to the drippings and sauté the peppers for about 10 minutes. Remove the peppers and set aside along with the meat. Add the pineapple juice, soy sauce, brown sugar, and instant coffee to the meat drippings and bring to a boil.

In a shaker container mix the cornstarch and water. Shake vigorously and add to the boiling sauce with a whisk. Serve the thickened sauce over rice, add a serving of meat, and top with peppers.

IRON	per serving heme iron MILLIGRAMS	nonheme iron MILLIGRAMS
	0.7	3.0

Tostidos

Serves 6 to 8

1	tablespoon olive oil
¼	cup finely chopped onion
1	tablespoon minced garlic
1	pound ground turkey
1	6-ounce can tomato paste
3	cans hot coffee (2¼ cups)
1	tablespoon cumin
1	teaspoon salt
2	tablespoons fresh chopped parsley
	Pinch red pepper
8	corn tortillas
1	cup healthy "refried" beans
1½	cups shredded Monterey Jack cheese
4	cups shredded lettuce
1	cup avocado topping

IS LOW IN HEME IRON AND CONTAINS

THIS RECIPE

substances that inhibit absorption of nonheme IRON	
X	calcium
X	dairy phosphate
	eggs
X	phytate phosphorus
X X	polyphenols tannic acid chlorogenic acid phenolic acid
	oxalates

In a saucepan heat the olive oil and sauté the onion and garlic. Add the meat and cook until the meat is done. Add the tomato paste, hot coffee, cumin, salt, parsley, and red pepper, and simmer until the mixture is thickened.

Preheat the oven to 350°. On each tortilla spread the refried beans. Add a layer of meat, and then cheese. Heat in the oven for 15 minutes. Remove and serve with shredded lettuce and avocado topping.

IRON	per serving	
	heme iron MILLIGRAMS	nonheme iron MILLIGRAMS
	0.3	2.5

Tuna Casserole

6 servings

2	quarts water
1	teaspoon salt
1	tea bag
12	ounces whole-wheat noodles
1	cup Mushroom Velouté (see recipe on page 205)
½	cup reduced fat sour cream
2	tablespoons mayonnaise
1	8-ounce can white water-packed tuna, drained
½	cup frozen peas
1	cup shredded Cheddar cheese

THIS RECIPE	IS LOW IN HEME IRON AND CONTAINS
	substances that inhibit absorption of nonheme IRON
X	calcium
X	dairy phosphate
	eggs
X	phytate phosphorus
X X	polyphenols tannic acid chlorogenic acid phenolic acid
	oxalates

In a stockpot bring the water, salt, and tea bag to a boil. Drop the noodles into the boiling water, and cook according to the time specified on the package. Drain and rinse the noodles.

In a medium bowl combine the velouté, sour cream, and mayonnaise.

Spray an 8-inch square glass baking dish with vegetable spray. Layer noodles, a portion of sauce, all of the tuna, then the peas. Cover with the remaining sauce and the Cheddar cheese. Bake uncovered at 350° for 45 minutes.

Note: Drinking tea or coffee with this meal is recommended.

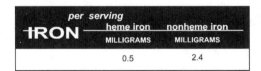

IRON	*per serving*	
	heme iron MILLIGRAMS	nonheme iron MILLIGRAMS
	0.5	2.4

Turkey Chili

Serves 4

1	tablespoon olive oil
½	cup finely chopped onion
1	pound fresh ground turkey
1	15¼-ounce can diced tomatoes
1	6-ounce can tomato paste
3	cans hot coffee (2¼ cups)
1	cup catsup
1	teaspoon salt
½	teaspoon red pepper
1	15¼-ounce can dark red kidney beans

IS LOW IN HEME IRON AND CONTAINS

THIS RECIPE

	substances that inhibit absorption of nonheme IRON
X	calcium
X	dairy phosphate
	eggs
X	phytate phosphorus
X X	polyphenols tannic acid chlorogenic acid phenolic acid
	oxalates

In a saucepan heat the oil and sauté the onion. Add the meat and cook until done. Add the tomatoes and simmer for 15 minutes. Add the tomato paste, hot coffee, catsup, and seasonings, and simmer for 30 minutes.

Rinse and drain the beans. Add to the chili and heat through.

Note: Drinking tea with this meal is recommended.

IRON	per serving heme iron MILLIGRAMS	nonheme iron MILLIGRAMS
	0.6	4.9

Turkey Florentine Noodle Casserole

Serves 8

1	1¾ pound turkey breast
1	cup brewed strong black tea
2	parsnips, washed and trimmed
2	ribs celery with leaves
1	cup diced fresh tomatoes
1½	teaspoons salt
2	tablespoons coarse ground black pepper
7	cups water
1½	cups brewed strong black tea
10	ounces spinach noodles
4	cups strained turkey stock
¼	cup olive oil
¼	cup all-purpose flour
1	cups heavy cream
1	teaspoon salt
1	cup freshly grated Parmesan cheese
¼	teaspoon nutmeg

THIS RECIPE IS LOW IN HEME IRON AND CONTAINS

substances that inhibit absorption of nonheme IRON

X	calcium
X	dairy phosphate
	eggs
X	phytate phosphorus
X X	polyphenols tannic acid chlorogenic acid phenolic acid
	oxalates

Place the turkey breast, 1 cup of tea, parsnips, celery, tomatoes, ½ teaspoon of salt, and pepper in a cooking bag. Close the bag and bake at 325° for 2 hours.

In a stockpot bring the water to a boil with 1 teaspoon of salt and the tea added, and cook the spinach noodles until almost done. Drain, rinse, and set aside.

When the turkey is done, remove it from the oven bag and let cool for slicing. Place ½ cup of turkey stock plus the cooked vegetables in a food processor. Pulse and set aside.

In a saucepan heat the olive oil and whisk in the flour until a paste forms. Slowly add ½ cup of stock, then the puréed vegetables. As the mixture thickens, continue to pour in the stock until the sauce is the consistency of very thick gravy. Whisk in the cream and nutmeg. Heat through but do not boil. Season with 1 teaspoon of salt.

In a 9 x 13-inch glass casserole dish layer the noodles and sliced turkey, and cover with the sauce. Top with Parmesan. Bake uncovered at 400° for about 20 minutes.

IRON	*per serving*	
	heme iron MILLIGRAMS	nonheme iron MILLIGRAMS
	0.4	2.2

Veal Paprikash
Serves 6

		IS LOW IN HEME IRON AND CONTAINS

	substances that inhibit absorption of nonheme
THIS RECIPE	**IRON**

	substance
X	calcium
X	dairy phosphate
	eggs
X	phytate phosphorus
X X	polyphenols tannic acid chlorogenic acid phenolic acid
	oxalates

¼   cup olive oil
1   pound veal, trimmed and cut into stew-size pieces
½   cup flour
½   cup finely chopped onion
1   tablespoon high-quality fresh ground paprika
½   cup chopped red bell pepper (green bell pepper if red is not available)
½   cup diced tomatoes
1   tablespoon tomato paste
1   cup brewed strong black tea
1   cup sour cream
    Tiny Dumplings (recipe below)

In a skillet heat the oil. Dredge the meat in flour and brown in the hot oil. Set the meat aside. Add the onion and sauté until tender. Add the paprika, pepper, tomatoes, paste, and tea. Bring to a gentle boil to thicken. Return the meat to the sauce and heat through. Stir in the sour cream. Serve over Tiny Dumplings.

TINY DUMPLINGS:
1   cup flour
½   teaspoon salt
½   cup brewed black tea
2   quarts water

Sift together the flour and salt. Add the tea, and mix until a dough forms. Place the dough on a floured pastry cloth and roll out until about ¼ inch thick. Cut into ½-inch wide strips, and cut each strip into ½-inch dumplings. Drop into boiling water. Dumplings will float when done. Scoop out and set aside.

Note: Drinking tea with this meal is recommended.

IRON	per serving	
	heme iron MILLIGRAMS	nonheme iron MILLIGRAMS
	0.7	2.3

Veal Moussaka

Serves 6

1	cup olive oil
1	eggplant
2	cups whole-wheat flour for dredging
2	eggs, lightly beaten
2	cups bread crumbs
2	tablespoons olive oil
¼	cup whole-wheat flour
1	teaspoon salt
¼	teaspoon white pepper
1	cup 1% milk
1	cup shredded Monterey Jack cheese
¼	cup grated Parmesan cheese
1	pound ground veal
2	cups Marinara Sauce (see recipe on page 204)
½	teaspoon cinnamon
½	teaspoon oregano
	Shredded Cheddar for topping
	Parmesan cheese for topping

THIS RECIPE IS LOW IN HEME IRON AND CONTAINS

	substances that inhibit absorption of nonheme **IRON**
X	calcium
X	dairy phosphate
X	eggs
X	phytate phosphorus
X X	polyphenols tannic acid chlorogenic acid phenolic acid
	oxalates

In a skillet heat 1 cup of olive oil over medium-high heat for frying.

Wash and dry the eggplant. Split the eggplant lengthwise, then again across into medium-width slices. In separate shallow dishes place 2 cups of whole-wheat flour, the eggs, and bread crumbs. Dredge the eggplant slices first in flour, then in the eggs, then in bread crumbs. Drop in hot olive oil, brown, turn and brown the other side.

Remove from the oil, and place on a paper towel to drain. Sprinkle salt lightly over the surface of the fried eggplant.

Prepare the cheese sauce. In a saucepan heat 2 tablespoons of olive oil. Whisk in ¼ cup of whole-wheat flour and add 1 teaspoon of salt and ¼ teaspoon of white pepper. Stir until light brown. Slowly add the milk, stirring until blended. Add the Monterey Jack and Parmesan cheeses, and heat until melted and smooth.

Prepare the meat sauce. In a skillet brown the veal. Drain and add the marinara sauce, cinnamon, and oregano.

Place the breaded eggplant in the bottom of a shallow glass casserole dish, overlapping each piece with the next. Cover with meat sauce, then cheese sauce. Top with shredded Cheddar and sprinkle with Parmesan. Bake uncovered at 350° for 45 minutes or until the top begins to brown.

†RON	per serving		
		heme iron	nonheme iron
		MILLIGRAMS	MILLIGRAMS
		0.36	2.2

Veal Stroganoff
Serves 6

1	**pound veal, cut into thick strips**
½	**cup hearty red wine (burgundy)**
½	**cup brewed black tea**
4	**tablespoons whole-wheat flour**
½	**cup olive oil**
½	**cup finely chopped onion**
1½	**cups sliced mushrooms**
1	**cup broth**
1	**cup sour cream**
	Cooked spinach noodles or wild rice

THIS RECIPE **IS LOW IN HEME IRON AND CONTAINS** substances that inhibit absorption of nonheme **IRON**

	calcium
X	dairy
	phosphate
	eggs
	phytate
	phosphorus
X	polyphenols
	tannic acid
	chlorogenic acid
	phenolic acid

In a shallow dish marinate the meat overnight in the wine and tea.

Dredge the meat in flour. In a skillet heat the olive oil and sauté the meat until browned. Remove the meat and sauté the onion for 10 to 15 minutes. Add the mushrooms and sauté until tender. Return the meat to the skillet and add the broth and marinade. Simmer until the meat is tender and the liquid is reduced by half. Stir in the sour cream and heat through.

Serve over cooked spinach noodles or wild rice.

Note: Drinking tea with this meal is recommended.

†RON	per serving		
		heme iron	nonheme iron
		MILLIGRAMS	MILLIGRAMS
		0.63	1.96

Vegetable Lasagna

Serves 8

IS LOW IN HEME IRON AND CONTAINS	

THIS RECIPE

	substances that inhibit absorption of nonheme IRON
X	calcium
X	dairy phosphate
X	eggs
X	phytate phosphorus
X X	polyphenols tannic acid chlorogenic acid phenolic acid
X	oxalates

2	cups chopped broccoli
1	tablespoon water
2	tablespoons olive oil
1	cup finely chopped onion
1	tablespoon minced garlic
1	cup sliced mushrooms
1	cup chopped green pepper
½	teaspoon salt
7	cups water
1	cup brewed strong black tea
1	teaspoon salt
9	medium width lasagna noodles
1	cup ricotta cheese
2	eggs
¼	cup fresh chopped parsley
½	teaspoon dried thyme, crushed
½	teaspoon dried marjoram, crushed
2	tablespoons capers
½	cup black olives
¼	teaspoon red pepper
1	cup shredded mozzarella cheese
4	cups Marinara Sauce (see recipe on page 204)
½	cup grated Parmesan cheese

Chop the broccoli into very small pieces. Place in a microwave safe glass bowl with 1 tablespoon of water. Cover with plastic wrap and cook on medium-high for 2 minutes or until tender.

In a skillet heat 2 tablespoons of oil and sauté the onion and minced garlic until tender, about 15 minutes. Add the mushrooms and cook until tender and no liquid remains.

Add the green pepper, and continue cooking about 5 to 7 minutes until the peppers are tender. Sprinkle the cooked vegetables with ½ teaspoon of salt.

In a stockpot bring the water, tea, and 1 teaspoon of salt to a boil. Drop the lasagna noodles into the boiling tea-water and cook until tender, about 10 minutes. Drain and rinse.

Mix together the ricotta cheese, egg, herbs, capers, olives, and red pepper.

Spray the bottom of a 9 x 13-inch glass baking dish with vegetable spray. Place 3 noodles lengthwise in the dish. Begin layers of cheese mixture, mushroom-onion mixture, then broccoli, and mozzarella. Spoon about ⅔ cup of marinara sauce over the layers and top with Parmesan cheese. Repeat with another layer in the same sequence, ending with a layer of noodles topped with sauce and Parmesan. Reserve additional sauce for individual servings.

Cover and bake at 375° for 30 minutes.

Uncover and bake an additional 10 minutes. Let stand for 10 to 15 minutes before serving.

IRON	per serving	
	heme iron MILLIGRAMS	nonheme iron MILLIGRAMS
	trace	1.56

Webb's "Faux Bacon"

Bacon does not contain much iron but it is high in fat. It offers great flavor to recipes and should not necessarily be eliminated from one's diet unless instructed to do so by a physician. One alternative to regular bacon is Webb's "faux bacon."

While owning and operating a very busy family restaurant sometimes the kitchen would run out of a product and there was not time to go to the store. Webb Garrison, husband of author Cheryl Garrison, often devised creative substitutes. During one such event when the kitchen ran out of bacon and several orders for club sandwiches needed to be filled, "faux bacon" was invented. Webb grabbed a slab of deli ham, sliced several pieces on the meat slicer then cut each piece into long strips similar to the shape of bacon. He then dropped the pieces into hot oil. Customers reported they enjoyed their club sandwiches and that the "bacon" was delicious.

Because olive oil is used as its fat, "faux bacon" is a bit healthier than regular bacon, though it contains about the same amount of sodium.

2   ounces very lean ham, thinly sliced
1   cup olive oil

For the best type of ham, look in the lunch meat section for reduced sodium/fat ham.

Cut the ham lengthwise into ½-inch-wide slices.

Method #1: Pour the olive oil into a shallow glass cooking dish. Place in a 425° oven until the oil is heated. Place strips of ham in the oil and return to the oven. Ham will fry just like regular bacon with sufficient oil and heat. For best results, be certain to get the oil very hot before adding the ham.

Method #2: In a skillet heat the olive oil. Place strips of ham in the hot oil. Ham will fry just like regular bacon with sufficient oil and heat.

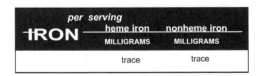

IRON	per serving heme iron MILLIGRAMS	nonheme iron MILLIGRAMS
	trace	trace

Side Dishes

Asparagus with Lemon Caraway Sauce
Serves 4

¾	pound fresh asparagus
1	cup tea
1	ounce fresh lemon juice
½	teaspoon caraway seed
1	tablespoon cornstarch
¼	cup sour cream
½	teaspoon salt
	Pinch white pepper

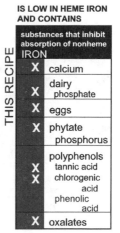

IS LOW IN HEME IRON AND CONTAINS

THIS RECIPE

substances that inhibit absorption of nonheme IRON

X	calcium
X	dairy phosphate
X	eggs
X	phytate phosphorus
X X	polyphenols tannic acid chlorogenic acid phenolic acid
X	oxalates

Wash the asparagus and snap off the woody ends. In a saucepan bring the tea to a boil with the lemon juice. Add the asparagus and caraway and simmer in the liquid until tender. Remove the asparagus and bring the liquid to a boil. In a shaker mix the cornstarch with a bit of water and shake to mix well. Add the cornstarch mixture to the cooking liquid and whisk constantly until thick. Add the sour cream. Season with salt and pepper.

IRON	per serving heme iron MILLIGRAMS	nonheme iron MILLIGRAMS
	trace	1.56

Artichoke Asparagus Casserole
Serves 4 to 6

1	egg, lightly beaten
½	cup egg substitute
1	3-ounce package Neufchatel cheese
¼	cup shredded Parmesan cheese
¾	teaspoon garlic powder
¼	teaspoon white pepper
¼	cup strong brewed tea
½	cup Pepperidge Farm brand stuffing mix
¾	cup shredded Swiss cheese
1	cup ricotta cheese
¾	cup shredded Vermont or New York sharp Cheddar cheese
1	small jar artichoke hearts
1	cup chopped frozen asparagus
1	tablespoon fresh chopped parsley
1	tablespoon oregano
1	2-ounce jar diced pimientos, drained

THIS RECIPE **IS LOW IN HEME IRON AND CONTAINS** substances that inhibit absorption of nonheme IRON:

X	calcium
X	dairy phosphate
X	eggs
X	phytate phosphorus
X X	polyphenols tannic acid chlorogenic acid phenolic acid

In a large bowl mix the egg, egg substitute, Neufchatel cheese, Parmesan cheese, garlic powder, and pepper. Add the tea, stuffing mix, Swiss, ricotta, and half the Cheddar cheese. Dice the artichoke hearts and add to the mixture along with the asparagus, parsley, oregano, and pimientos.

Spray a glass casserole dish with vegetable spray and place the mixture in the dish. Bake at 350° for about 30 minutes.

Top with the remaining Cheddar cheese and bake for an additional 10 to 15 minutes. Let stand for 10 minutes before serving.

IRON per serving	heme iron MILLIGRAMS	nonheme iron MILLIGRAMS
	trace	1.97

Baked Beans

Serves 4

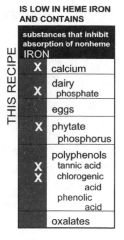

**IS LOW IN HEME IRON
AND CONTAINS**

	substances that inhibit absorption of nonheme
	IRON
X	calcium
X	dairy phosphate
	eggs
X	phytate phosphorus
X X	polyphenols tannic acid chlorogenic acid phenolic acid
	oxalates

THIS RECIPE

⅓	cup brown sugar
½	cup strong coffee
¼	cup vinegar
1	cup catsup
1	teaspoon dry mustard
1	28-ounce can pork and beans, drained
½	cup chopped onion

In a saucepan combine the brown sugar, coffee, vinegar, catsup, and dry mustard, and simmer for 5 to 10 minutes.

In a casserole dish layer the beans, onions, and sauce mixture. Cover and bake at 350° for 40 minutes.

Uncover and bake at 400° for 20 minutes.

Remove from the oven and let stand 10 minutes before serving.

IRON	per serving	
	heme iron MILLIGRAMS	nonheme iron MILLIGRAMS
	0.0	2.5

Baked Beets with Apple Glaze
Serves 4

1	**bunch fresh beets**
1	**cup apple juice**
1	**teaspoon cornstarch**

Rinse the beets well and cut off the stems and roots. Do not discard the stems; use in vegetable broth or in compost.

Preheat the oven to 350°. Place the beets in a glass cooking dish and bake uncovered for about 1 hour; a fork or knife will slide in easily when the beet is done.

In a saucepan bring the apple juice to a boil. In a shaker mix the cornstarch with a bit of water and shake to mix well. Add the cornstarch mixture to the apple juice and whisk constantly until thick. Remove the beets from the oven and top with the apple glaze.

THIS RECIPE	IS LOW IN HEME IRON AND CONTAINS	
	substances that inhibit absorption of nonheme IRON	
		calcium
		dairy phosphate
		eggs
	X	phytate phosphorus
		polyphenols tannic acid chlorogenic acid
	X	phenolic acid
		oxalates

+RON	per serving	
	heme iron MILLIGRAMS	nonheme iron MILLIGRAMS
	0.0	0.7

Baked Rice

Serves 6 to 8

¼   cup olive oil
¼   cup finely chopped onion
1   teaspoon minced garlic
½   cup chopped fresh tomatoes
2   cups chicken broth
1   cup brewed tea
1   teaspoon salt
     Pinch red pepper
1½   cups uncooked basmati rice
½   cup finely chopped spinach
¼   cup chopped fresh parsley
2   sprigs thyme or ½ teaspoon dried thyme
1   bay leaf

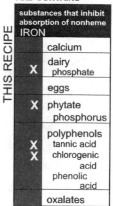

THIS RECIPE	IS LOW IN HEME IRON AND CONTAINS	
	substances that inhibit absorption of nonheme IRON	
		calcium
	X	dairy phosphate
		eggs
	X	phytate phosphorus
	X X	polyphenols tannic acid chlorogenic acid phenolic acid
		oxalates

Preheat the oven to 400°. In a skillet heat the oil and sauté the onion and garlic until golden. Add the tomatoes and cook until tender.

Add the broth, tea, salt, pepper, rice, spinach, parsley, thyme, and bay leaf. Cover and bake at 425° for 40 minutes.

Turn off the oven and let stand without opening the oven door for 20 to 30 minutes.

Remove the bay leaf before serving.

IRON	per serving	
	heme iron MILLIGRAMS	nonheme iron MILLIGRAMS
	0.0	2.1

Broccoli Casserole

Serves 4

1	10-ounce box chopped broccoli, thawed but not cooked (leftover broccoli works fine also)
1	cup cooked rice, (prepared in broth-tea mixture or use leftover baked rice)
½	cup cottage cheese
1	cup Hollandaise sauce (Knorr Swiss brand, 1 package prepared)
1	cup shredded sharp Cheddar cheese
1	egg
1	tablespoon flour
1	teaspoon salt
½	teaspoon white pepper

Preheat the oven to 350°. In a large bowl combine all of the ingredients. Lightly oil a glass baking dish and pour the mixture into the dish. Bake for 45 minutes.

Let stand 10 minutes before serving.

THIS RECIPE IS LOW IN HEME IRON AND CONTAINS

substances that inhibit absorption of nonheme **IRON**

X	calcium
X	dairy phosphate
	eggs
X	phytate phosphorus
X X	polyphenols tannic acid chlorogenic acid phenolic acid
X	oxalates

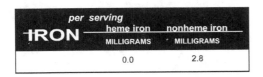

IRON	*per serving*	
	heme iron MILLIGRAMS	nonheme iron MILLIGRAMS
	0.0	2.8

Brussels Sprouts with Sour Cream and Dill

Serves 4

2	cups fresh Brussels sprouts
1	cup brewed tea
1	cup sour cream
	Pinch black pepper
1	teaspoon dill weed

Wash the sprouts and cut off the stems. Steam in tea until done, about 40 minutes (tender when pierced with a fork).

In a saucepan heat the sour cream and pepper, and add the dill. Serve over the Brussels sprouts.

IS LOW IN HEME IRON AND CONTAINS

THIS RECIPE

substances that inhibit absorption of nonheme IRON	
	calcium
X	dairy phosphate
	eggs
X	phytate phosphorus
X X	polyphenols tannic acid chlorogenic acid phenolic acid
	oxalates

IRON — *per serving*

heme iron MILLIGRAMS	nonheme iron MILLIGRAMS
0.0	0.5

Cabbage and Onions with Black Pepper

Serves 4

½	cup olive oil
½	yellow onion finely, chopped
½	head green cabbage, chopped
½	teaspoon salt
	Black pepper
½	cup brewed tea

In a skillet heat the oil and sauté the onion until tender. Increase the heat and add the cabbage. Stir so the onion is mixed with the cabbage. Add salt to taste and generous amounts of black pepper. Add the tea, cover, and steam for 30 minutes.

IS LOW IN HEME IRON AND CONTAINS

THIS RECIPE

substances that inhibit absorption of nonheme IRON	
	calcium
X	dairy phosphate
	eggs
X	phytate phosphorus
X X	polyphenols tannic acid chlorogenic acid phenolic acid
	oxalates

IRON — *per serving*

heme iron MILLIGRAMS	nonheme iron MILLIGRAMS
0.0	0.3

Cabbage Casserole
Serves 4

2	tablespoons olive oil
½	cup finely chopped onion
½	head green cabbage, chopped
1	cup brewed tea
½	teaspoon salt
½	teaspoon black pepper
¼	teaspoon caraway seeds
1	egg
½	cup light cream
⅔	cup seasoned bread stuffing
⅔	cup shredded Swiss cheese
¼	cup Parmesan cheese

THIS RECIPE

IS LOW IN HEME IRON AND CONTAINS

substances that inhibit absorption of nonheme IRON

X	calcium
X	dairy phosphate
X	eggs
X	phytate phosphorus
X X	polyphenols tannic acid chlorogenic acid phenolic acid
	oxalates

In a stockpot heat the olive oil and sauté the onion until tender. Add the cabbage and tea, and cook the until the cabbage is tender. Add salt, pepper, and caraway seeds.

In a medium bowl combine the egg and cream. In an oiled glass 8-inch square baking dish layer the cabbage onion mixture, then stuffing, then Swiss cheese, reserving a small amount to put on top. Pour the cream mixture over the top. Sprinkle with the remaining Swiss and Parmesan cheeses. Bake uncovered at 350° for about 40 minutes.

IRON — per serving

heme iron MILLIGRAMS	nonheme iron MILLIGRAMS
0.0	0.5

Clam Spread

Serves 4

2   tablespoons canned minced clams, drained and rinsed
1   tablespoon apple juice
4   ounces Neufchatel cheese
¼   cup diced Velveeta cheese
1   tablespoon finely chopped onion
1   tablespoon finely chopped green pepper
1   teaspoon Worcestershire sauce
      Pinch red pepper

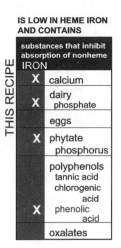

THIS RECIPE	IS LOW IN HEME IRON AND CONTAINS
	substances that inhibit absorption of nonheme IRON
X	calcium
X	dairy phosphate
	eggs
X	phytate phosphorus
	polyphenols tannic acid chlorogenic acid
X	phenolic acid
	oxalates

In a food processor combine all of the ingredients. Pulse until well blended.

Spread on melba toast rounds and place under the broiler to heat.

Note: This recipe calls for a very small amount of clams due to the high heme iron content. Substances in this recipe that inhibit the absorption of iron include phenolic acid, phytate phosphorus, phosphates, calcium.

IRON	*per serving*	
	heme iron MILLIGRAMS	nonheme iron MILLIGRAMS
	0.2	0.4

Crab Spread

Serves 4

1	cup chopped imitation crab
1	tablespoon apple juice
1	spring onion, chopped
1	8-ounce package Neufchatel cheese
	Pinch red pepper
2	tablespoons chopped fresh parsley
1	tablespoon finely chopped onion

In a large bowl combine all of the ingredients with hands. Refrigerate until chilled.

Serve chilled on saltine crackers.

THIS RECIPE IS LOW IN HEME IRON AND CONTAINS

	substances that inhibit absorption of nonheme IRON
X	calcium
X	dairy phosphate
X	eggs
X	phytate phosphorus
X X	polyphenols tannic acid chlorogenic acid phenolic acid
	oxalates

IRON	*per serving*	
	heme iron MILLIGRAMS	nonheme iron MILLIGRAMS
	0.0	0.5

Confetti Vegetable Casserole
Serves 4 to 6

1	tablespoon olive oil
½	cup finely chopped onion
2	tablespoons minced garlic
1	cup sliced fresh mushrooms
½	cup brown rice
½	cup wild rice
1	teaspoon salt
½	teaspoon white pepper
1½	cups turkey or chicken broth
½	cup brewed tea
¼	cup shredded carrot
¼	cup chopped fresh spinach
½	cup frozen asparagus pieces (thawed but not cooked)
½	cup diced tomato
2	tablespoons fresh chopped parsley
1	egg, lightly beaten
2	tablespoons whole-wheat flour
1	cup cubed havarti cheese
¼	cup grated Parmesan cheese
2	cups Mushroom Velouté (see recipe on page 205)

THIS RECIPE IS LOW IN HEME IRON AND CONTAINS substances that inhibit absorption of nonheme **IRON**

X	calcium
X	dairy phosphate
X	eggs
X	phytate phosphorus
X X	polyphenols tannic acid chlorogenic acid phenolic acid
	oxalates

In a skillet heat the olive oil and sauté the onion and garlic until tender. Add the mushrooms and cook until tender. Add the rices, salt, white pepper, broth, and tea, and bring to a boil. Cover, reduce the heat, and allow the rice to steam for 25 minutes (brown rice may take longer).

In a large mixing bowl combine the vegetables, parsley, egg, and flour. Add the rice, cheeses, and velouté.

Spray a casserole dish with vegetable spray. Pack the ingredients into the casserole dish. Bake at 350° for 45 minutes or until the center puffs up and begins to brown.

IRON	per serving	
	heme iron MILLIGRAMS	nonheme iron MILLIGRAMS
	0.0	0.5

Dressing (Stuffing)

Serves 10 to 12

¼	cup olive oil
½	cup finely chopped onion
½	cup chopped celery
6	cups whole-wheat bread cubes
4	cups leftover corn bread (tear apart and let stand in open air overnight)
2	tablespoons chopped fresh parsley
3	cups turkey or chicken broth
1	cup brewed tea
2	tablespoons salt
4	tablespoons rubbed sage
1	teaspoon black pepper
2	eggs, lightly beaten

IS LOW IN HEME IRON AND CONTAINS

THIS RECIPE	substances that inhibit absorption of nonheme IRON	
		calcium
	X	dairy phosphate
	X	eggs
	X	phytate phosphorus
	X	polyphenols tannic acid
	X	chlorogenic acid
		phenolic acid
	X	oxalates

In a skillet heat the oil and sauté the onion and celery until tender. In a large bowl stir all of the ingredients together, adding the eggs last. Pack into a glass baking dish. Bake at 375° for 45 minutes.

Let stand 10 minutes before serving.

IRON	*per serving*	
	heme iron MILLIGRAMS	nonheme iron MILLIGRAMS
	0.2	3.15

Dried Beans

Serves 4 to 6

8	cups broth
2	cups brewed tea
1	pound dried beans (navy, pinto, black, lima, or any personal favorite)
1	teaspoon salt

In a stockpot bring to a boil the broth, tea, and beans. Reduce the heat and simmer the beans for 1 hour.

Add the salt and continue cooking the beans until tender.

THIS RECIPE IS LOW IN HEME IRON AND CONTAINS

substances that inhibit absorption of nonheme IRON

	calcium
X	dairy phosphate
	eggs
X	phytate phosphorus
X X	polyphenols tannic acid chlorogenic acid phenolic acid
	oxalates

IRON — *per serving*

	heme iron MILLIGRAMS	nonheme iron MILLIGRAMS
	0.0	2.4

Funny Fries

THIS RECIPE

IS LOW IN HEME IRON AND CONTAINS

substances that inhibit absorption of nonheme IRON
calcium
dairy phosphate
eggs
X phytate phosphorus
polyphenols tannic acid chlorogenic acid phenolic acid
oxalates

According to the National Cancer Institute, in the United States between the years 1970 and 1994, per-person consumption of vegetables increased by 19 percent. The potato topped the list of favorite vegetables. Unfortunately more than 50 percent of potatoes eaten are consumed as French fries, which joins the ranks of soft drinks, candy and refined sugar as unhealthy foods Americans consume in excess.

Potatoes are rich in fiber, with a whopping 4 grams per cup when eaten with the skins. They also contain calcium, magnesium, potassium, and folate. Prepared with olive oil, which is high in monounsaturated fat—the good kind of fat—potatoes with skins offer a healthy alternative to deep-fat-fried potatoes.

1   **dozen new (red) potatoes**
¼   **cup olive oil**
    Salt to taste

Wash and cut the potatoes in half; place in cold water to preserve. Oil the bottom of a large shallow glass baking dish. Shake salt onto the oil.

Preheat the oven to 450°. Place the dish in the oven to heat the oil (about 5 to 7 minutes once the oven is at temperature). Dry the potatoes with paper towels. Remove the dish from the oven. Place the potatoes face down in the hot oil. Return to the oven and bake for 15 to 20 minutes. The meat side of the potato should be golden brown, not black. Cut off the oven and let the potatoes stand in the oven for about 20 minutes.

IRON	*per serving*	
	heme iron MILLIGRAMS	**nonheme iron** MILLIGRAMS
	trace	2.1

Herbed Olive Oil with Crusty French Bread
Serves 4

1	**loaf French bread**
½	**cup extra virgin olive oil**
1	**tablespoon spicy mustard**
1	**tablespoon fresh parsley**
¼	**teaspoon fresh cracked pepper**

THIS RECIPE	IS LOW IN HEME IRON AND CONTAINS
	substances that inhibit absorption of nonheme IRON
	calcium
	dairy phosphate
	eggs
X	phytate phosphorus
	polyphenols tannic acid chlorogenic acid phenolic acid
	oxalates

Bake the bread uncovered at 375° until crusty and brown, about 10 to 15 minutes. In a small bowl combine the olive oil, mustard, parsley, and pepper. Place the crusty hot bread and olive oil for dipping on the dinner table. Tear off pieces of bread and dip in olive oil.

IRON	per serving heme iron MILLIGRAMS	nonheme iron MILLIGRAMS
	0.0	0.6

Hungarian Cheese Spread
Serves 4

¼ cup (½ stick) butter, softened
1 package cream cheese, softened
1 tablespoon caraway seed
1 tablespoon ground paprika
1 tablespoon chives
1 teaspoon dry mustard
2 tablespoons finely chopped green pepper
¼ cup chopped radishes

In a medium bowl combine all of the ingredients. Serve chilled on saltine crackers or rye or wheat bread.

THIS RECIPE	IS LOW IN HEME IRON AND CONTAINS	
	substances that inhibit absorption of nonheme IRON	
	X	calcium
	X	dairy phosphate
		eggs
	X	phytate phosphorus
		polyphenols tannic acid chlorogenic acid phenolic acid
	X	oxalates

IRON	per serving	
	heme iron MILLIGRAMS	nonheme iron MILLIGRAMS
	0.0	trace

Italian Green Bean Casserole
Serves 8

2	14.5-ounce cans Italian cut green beans, drained
⅓	teaspoon oregano
⅓	cup Parmesan cheese
½	cup light cream
1	cup Mushroom Velouté (see recipe on page 205)
1	cup Pepperidge Farm brand bread stuffing mix

In a medium bowl mix the beans, oregano, Parmesan, cream, and
velouté.

Spray a glass casserole dish with vegetable spray. Distribute
half the stuffing mix over the bottom. Pour the beans and sauce over the stuffing mix.
Top with the remaining stuffing mix. Bake at 400° for 40 minutes.

THIS RECIPE

IS LOW IN HEME IRON AND CONTAINS

substances that inhibit absorption of nonheme IRON	
X	calcium
X	dairy phosphate
	eggs
X	phytate phosphorus
X X	polyphenols tannic acid chlorogenic acid phenolic acid
	oxalates

IRON	*per serving*	
	heme iron MILLIGRAMS	nonheme iron MILLIGRAMS
	trace	0.8

Kohlrabi Alfredo with Cracked Pepper
Serves 4

2	to 3 kohlrabi bulbs
1	cup brewed tea
1	cup Alfredo sauce
1	teaspoon coarse ground or fresh cracked black pepper

In a steamer place the kohlrabi bulbs and steam in the tea until
tender. Cut the bulbs in half and spoon the Alfredo sauce over the
kohlrabi. Sprinkle generously with fresh ground black pepper.

THIS RECIPE

IS LOW IN HEME IRON AND CONTAINS

substances that inhibit absorption of nonheme IRON	
X	calcium
X	dairy phosphate
	eggs
X	phytate phosphorus
X X	polyphenols tannic acid chlorogenic acid phenolic acid
	oxalates

IRON	*per serving*	
	heme iron MILLIGRAMS	nonheme iron MILLIGRAMS
	0.0	0.3

Kasha and Bowties with Chopped Kale

Serving size: 1 cup

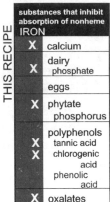

THIS RECIPE

IS LOW IN HEME IRON AND CONTAINS

	substances that inhibit absorption of nonheme
	IRON
X	calcium
X	dairy phosphate
	eggs
X	phytate phosphorus
X X	polyphenols tannic acid chlorogenic acid phenolic acid
X	oxalates

6	ounces bowtie pasta
7	cups water
1	teaspoon instant tea
1	teaspoon salt
2	tablespoons olive oil
1	cup finely chopped onion
1	teaspoon minced garlic
1	cup sliced mushrooms
1	cup chopped kale
1	teaspoon salt and black pepper
1	egg
1	cup kasha
2	cups hot chicken broth
1	teaspoon instant tea

In a stockpot cook the pasta in salted boiling water and the tea for about 8 minutes or until al dente. Drain, rinse, and set aside.

In a skillet heat the olive oil and sauté the onion and garlic for 15 minutes. Add the mushrooms and sauté until the liquid evaporates. Add the kale, and season with salt and pepper. Cover and cook until the kale is done.

In a mixing bowl beat the egg and stir in the kasha, mixing until all kernels are coated.

In a glass skillet on medium-high heat cook the kasha, stirring constantly until the grains are toasted. Add the hot broth and tea, and simmer for about 8 minutes. Do not overcook or the kasha will become mushy. Add the pasta and the kale mixture, and mix well.

IRON	*per serving*	
	heme iron MILLIGRAMS	nonheme iron MILLIGRAMS
	trace	1.2

Lima Bean Casserole

Serves 6 to 8

½	pound dry baby limas
7	cups water plus 1 cup brewed tea
1	teaspoon salt
2	strips bacon
1	tablespoon olive oil
¼	cup finely chopped onion
½	cup sour cream
1	cup Mushroom Velouté (see recipe on page 205)
¼	cup Parmesan cheese

THIS RECIPE IS LOW IN HEME IRON AND CONTAINS

	substances that inhibit absorption of nonheme IRON
X	calcium
X	dairy phosphate
	eggs
X	phytate phosphorus
X X	polyphenols tannic acid chlorogenic acid phenolic acid
	oxalates

In a stockpot simmer the limas in the water and tea seasoned with salt until tender.

Microwave the bacon strips until very crisp, drain, and set aside.

In a skillet heat the olive oil and sauté the onion until translucent. In a small bowl mix the sour cream and mushroom velouté, and add to the onion. Spray a square glass baking dish with vegetable spray. In the bottom of the dish layer limas, then sauce. Top with Parmesan and crumbled bacon. Bake uncovered at 350° for 45 minutes.

IRON	per serving	
	heme iron MILLIGRAMS	nonheme iron MILLIGRAMS
	trace	3.2

Macaroni and Cheese

Serves 8

1	16-ounce box whole-wheat elbow noodles
7	cups water
1	cup brewed tea
1	teaspoon salt
1	tablespoon olive oil
2	tablespoons oat bran blend flour
1	cup low fat milk
½	cup diced Velveeta cheese
½	cup shredded sharp Cheddar

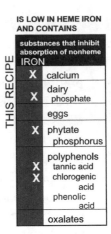

In a large pot cook the elbow noodles in the water and tea with salt until tender.

In the top of a double boiler over simmering water heat the olive oil. Add the oat bran flour and beat with a whisk until blended. Add the milk and continue to beat with a whisk until thickened. Add the Velveeta and Cheddar and gently mix. Whisk vigorously, scraping bottom edges gently with a wooden spoon. Pour the cheese sauce over cooked and rinsed macaroni. Cover and bake at 350° for 40 minutes.

Drink tea or coffee with this meal.

†RON	per serving heme iron MILLIGRAMS	nonheme iron MILLIGRAMS
	trace	3.2

Okra with Lime Sauce

Serves 6

1	pound okra
½	cup brewed tea
½	teaspoon salt
2	tablespoons milk
3	ounces Neufchatel cheese, cut into cubes
1	ounce fresh lime juice

Wash the okra and cut off the stems. Steam in tea and salt.

In a separate pan heat the milk. Add the cheese and warm until melted. Add the lime juice and whisk until blended. Top steamed okra with the lime sauce.

THIS RECIPE IS LOW IN HEME IRON AND CONTAINS

	substances that inhibit absorption of nonheme IRON
X	calcium
X	dairy phosphate
	eggs
X	phytate phosphorus
X	polyphenols tannic acid
X	chlorogenic acid
	phenolic acid
X	oxalates

IRON	per serving	
	heme iron MILLIGRAMS	nonheme iron MILLIGRAMS
	0.0	0.4

Pasta

Serves 4

1   cup flour
1   teaspoon salt
1   egg
7   cups broth
1   cup brewed tea
¼   teaspoon salt

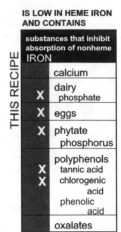

In a medium bowl combine the flour and salt. Place the flour mixture on a pastry cloth and create a well in the center. Break the egg into the well and blend the flour into the egg. Knead slightly, but do not overmix. Press the pasta down and sprinkle with flour. Dust the rolling pin with flour and roll out the pasta into thin sheets (get the sheets as thin as possible). Let dry for 2 hours.

Cut into 4-inch-wide strips. If the centers are still damp allow the pasta to dry another hour.

Stack the strips and beginning at one end cut ¼-inch-wide noodles. Toss with flour and drop into boiling broth with tea and salt. Simmer until tender, about 20 minutes.

IRON	*per serving*	
	heme iron	nonheme iron
	MILLIGRAMS	MILLIGRAMS
	0.2	0.5

Red Beans and Rice

Serves 4 to 6

7	cups water
	Ham bone with ½ cup ham pieces
1	pound red beans
2	cups brewed tea
1	teaspoon salt
1½	cups broth
½	cup brewed tea
1	teaspoon salt
1	teaspoon olive oil
1	cup rice
	Chopped spring onions

IS LOW IN HEME IRON AND CONTAINS

THIS RECIPE

	substances that inhibit absorption of nonheme IRON
	calcium
X	dairy phosphate
	eggs
X	phytate phosphorus
X	polyphenols tannic acid
X	chlorogenic acid
	phenolic acid
	oxalates

In a large pot bring the water to a boil. Add the ham bone, ham, beans, and 2 cups of tea. Reduce the heat and simmer the beans for 1 hour.

Add the salt and continue cooking the beans until tender.

In a separate pot bring the broth and ½ cup of tea to boil and add the salt, oil, and rice. Cover and steam for 25 minutes.

Spoon the beans over the rice. Top with chopped spring onions and serve with corn bread.

IRON	*per serving* heme iron MILLIGRAMS	nonheme iron MILLIGRAMS
	0.2	4.5

Red Oven Roasted Potatoes with Rosemary

Serves 4 to 6

12	red potatoes
	Olive oil
	Salt and pepper
2	tablespoons butter, melted
3	tablespoons olive oil
1	cup sour cream
2	tablespoons fresh rosemary
2	tablespoons chives
	Salt and pepper

THIS RECIPE IS LOW IN HEME IRON AND CONTAINS

substances that inhibit absorption of nonheme **IRON**

	calcium
X	dairy phosphate
	eggs
X	phytate phosphorus
	polyphenols tannic acid chlorogenic acid phenolic acid
	oxalates

Wash and cut the potatoes into halves. Preheat the oven to 400°. Coat a cookie sheet with olive oil, and lightly sprinkle with salt and pepper.

Place the cookie sheet in the oven for about 5 minutes until hot. Place the red potatoes cut side down on the hot sheet. Bake for 20 to 25 minutes until the potatoes are done (pierce with a fork).

While the potatoes are baking prepare the sauce. In a small saucepan over low heat combine the butter, oil, and sour cream. Add the rosemary and chives. Pour the sauce over the roasted potatoes. Season with salt and pepper to taste.

Potatoes prepared this way are a great substitute for French fries.

Drink tea or coffee with this meal.

IRON	per serving heme iron MILLIGRAMS	nonheme iron MILLIGRAMS
	0.0	2.3

Refried Beans

Makes 6 1-cup servings

1	**pound pinto beans**
2	**quarts water**
1	**tablespoon instant coffee**
2	**ounces country ham**
2	**tablespoons olive oil**
	Pinch red pepper

IS LOW IN HEME IRON AND CONTAINS

THIS RECIPE	substances that inhibit absorption of nonheme IRON	
		calcium
	X	dairy phosphate
		eggs
	X	phytate phosphorus
	X X	polyphenols tannic acid chlorogenic acid phenolic acid
		oxalates

Rinse and clean the beans thoroughly. Bring the beans to a boil in the water. Add the coffee and ham, boil for 10 minutes, then reduce the heat to simmer. Cover and slow cook for 2 hours.

Check each 40 minutes or so to assure adequate liquid still remains.

Remove the ham and cool the beans. Taste the beans for saltiness. (*Note:* Country ham is very salty; if another type of ham is used salt may have to be added for seasoning.)

In a food processor purée the beans. Drizzle the oil into the mixture. Add the red pepper. Add remaining liquid as needed to keep a paste-like texture.

IRON	*per serving*	
	heme iron	nonheme iron
	MILLIGRAMS	MILLIGRAMS
	trace	4.5

Shiitaki Mushrooms with Feta Cheese and Herbs

Serves 4

		IS LOW IN HEME IRON AND CONTAINS

THIS RECIPE		substances that inhibit absorption of nonheme IRON
	X	calcium
	X	dairy phosphate
		eggs
	X	phytate phosphorus
	X	polyphenols tannic acid chlorogenic acid phenolic acid
	X	oxalates

1   tablespoon olive oil
12   cleaned shiitaki mushrooms
1   teaspoon rosemary
1   teaspoon fresh chopped parsley
1   teaspoon chopped chives
        Pinch red pepper
½   cup feta cheese

Brush olive oil on the mushrooms and sprinkle with herbs. Place under the broiler for 5 to 7 minutes. Remove and sprinkle with red pepper and feta cheese.

†RON	per serving	
	heme iron MILLIGRAMS	nonheme iron MILLIGRAMS
	0.0	0.4

Shoepeg Corn with Roasted Red Peppers Neufchatel

Serves 6

¼   red bell pepper
1   tablespoon olive oil
1   10-ounce package frozen white shoepeg corn
½   cup brewed tea
3   ounces Neufchatel cheese

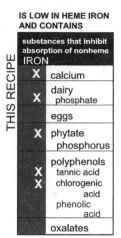

THIS RECIPE IS LOW IN HEME IRON AND CONTAINS substances that inhibit absorption of nonheme IRON

X	calcium
X	dairy phosphate
	eggs
X	phytate phosphorus
X X	polyphenols tannic acid chlorogenic acid phenolic acid
	oxalates

Wash and seed the red pepper quarter. Brush the pepper quarter with olive oil and cut into thin strips. Place under the broiler until roasted (3 to 4 minutes; the pepper will be charred). Allow to cool.

In a steamer pot steam the corn in the tea. Chop the Neufchatel and drop it into the corn. Chop the red pepper and add to the corn. Heat until the cheese melts.

IRON	per serving heme iron MILLIGRAMS	nonheme iron MILLIGRAMS
	0.0	0.6

Spinach Casserole

Serves 6

2	tablespoons olive oil
½	cup minced onion
2	eggs
½	cup lowfat milk
2	tablespoons chopped parsley
½	teaspoon salt
¼	teaspoon white pepper
½	cup cream cheese
1½	pounds fresh spinach
1½	cups rice
1	cup Swiss cheese (reserve ¼ cup for topping)
4	strips bacon, cooked and crumbled

IS LOW IN HEME IRON AND CONTAINS

THIS RECIPE

substances that inhibit absorption of nonheme IRON

	calcium
X	dairy phosphate
	eggs
	phytate phosphorus
	polyphenols tannic acid chlorogenic acid phenolic acid
X	oxalates

In a skillet heat the oil and sauté the onion. In a medium bowl beat the eggs. Add the milk, onion, parsley, salt, and pepper. Add the cream cheese, spinach, rice, and ¾ cup of Swiss cheese, and pour into a greased shallow baking dish. Top with the remaining cheese and bacon. Bake uncovered at 350° for 40 to 45minutes.

Let stand before serving.

IRON	*per serving* heme iron MILLIGRAMS	nonheme iron MILLIGRAMS
	trace	0.9

Squash Casserole

Serves 8 to 10

3	pounds yellow squash
4	tablespoons olive oil
1	medium onion, coarsely chopped
1	teaspoon salt
¼	teaspoon white pepper
1	cup brewed tea
2	cups Mushroom Velouté (see recipe on page 205 or 1 small can cream of mushroom soup)
1	cup reduced fat sour cream
1½	cups extra sharp Cheddar cheese (Vermont or New York)
2	cups Pepperidge Farm brand stuffing mix

THIS RECIPE IS LOW IN HEME IRON AND CONTAINS

substances that inhibit absorption of nonheme IRON	
	calcium
X	dairy phosphate
	eggs
	phytate phosphorus
X	polyphenols tannic acid chlorogenic acid phenolic acid
	oxalates

Preheat the oven to 350°. Rinse the squash, remove the stems, cut up, and set aside.

In a skillet heat the oil and sauté the onion until tender. Add the squash, salt, pepper and tea, and simmer until tender.

Lightly oil a baking dish with olive oil or vegetable spray.

In a medium bowl mix the mushroom velouté and sour cream.

In the prepared baking dish alternate layers of squash-onion mixture, then sauce, Cheddar cheese, and Pepperidge Farm brand stuffing mix. Continue layering, ending with stuffing mix as topping. Bake uncovered for 45 minutes.

IRON	per serving	
	heme iron MILLIGRAMS	nonheme iron MILLIGRAMS
	0.4	0.24

Twice Baked Potato

Serves 4

		IS LOW IN HEME IRON AND CONTAINS
		substances that inhibit absorption of nonheme
THIS RECIPE		IRON
		calcium
	X	dairy phosphate
		eggs
	X	phytate phosphorus
	X X	polyphenols tannic acid chlorogenic acid phenolic acid
	X	oxalates

4	Idaho baking potatoes
2	tablespoons hot water
1	tablespoon instant tea
½	cup sour cream
¼	cup finely chopped onion
1	tablespoon chives
1	teaspoon salt
	Pinch black pepper
⅔	cup cubed Velveeta cheese

Wash the potatoes and bake at 350° for 1 hour.

Remove, cool, and cut off the top, creating a shoe. Scoop out the potato meat and place in a bowl.

In a separate bowl mix the water and tea, and stir in the sour cream. Blend well. Add the sour cream mixture, onion, chives, salt, pepper, and Velveeta to the potato meat. Combine well and spoon back into the shells. Cover loosely and rebake at 300° for about 30 to 40 minutes.

Let stand 10 to 15 minutes before serving.

IRON	*per serving* heme iron MILLIGRAMS	nonheme iron MILLIGRAMS
	0.0	1.1

SAUCES

Sauces provide body and taste to recipes. When made in the traditional way with butter and cream, sauces undoubtedly add calories and animal fat to a recipe. Eliminating sauces from one's diet is not necessary. For persons who are in good health, exercise regularly, and incorporate variety into their diet, traditional butter and cream sauces can be enjoyed from time to time. For those who must reduce the amount of animal fat in their diet or reduce both fat and calories, reducing the consumption of rich sauces is one way to achieve this diet goal.

Most sauces are made with a combination of fat and flour, called a roux, to which broth is added. The roux mixture thickens the sauce, although some cooks use cornstarch as a thickening agent, especially for oriental recipes or fruit desserts. In *Cooking with Less Iron* a roux using olive oil as the fat in combination with oat blend, whole-wheat, rice bran, barley, soy, or buckwheat flour provides a healthy basis for sauces and gravies. Olive oil is rich in monounsaturated fat, the type that contributes to good health. Whole-grain flours are an excellent source of phytate, which impairs iron absorption.

Some sauces can be made with low fat mayonnaise and sour cream substitutes. Reduced fat mayonnaise and reduced fat sour cream are available commercially. Hellman's makes an excellent reduced fat mayonnaise. Breakstone makes an excellent reduced fat sour cream. Since tastes vary within families, sometimes it is more economical to make your own blends; below are some easy reduced fat recipes:

Reduced fat sour cream: Mix plain yogurt with regular sour cream 2:1. This reduces the amount of fat while maintaining the flavor and texture of sour cream.

Reduced fat mayonnaise #1: In a blender mix 1 cup Hellman's brand mayonnaise and ¼ cup brewed tea. Tea will discolor mayo but not change the taste significantly. Refrigerate to thicken.

Reduced fat mayo spread #2: In a blender combine ½ cup Hellman's brand mayonnaise, ¼ cup spicy mustard, ⅓ cup liquid lecithin, 1¼ teaspoons balsamic vinegar, 1 teaspoon of instant tea, ¼ to ½ teaspoon of salt, and ⅓ cup of olive oil. Combine all ingredients in a blender. Refrigerate to thicken. *Note:* Lecithin when taken daily can help reduce LDL cholesterol. Lecithin has a strong taste and will cause the spread to have a yellow color. Herbs such as basil, oregano, marjoram, chives, chervil, etc., can be added to this spread to give it extra zest.

Avocado Dip

Yield 2½ cups; serving size: ¼ cup

¼   cup chopped onion
2   avocado, peeled and seed removed
2   tablespoons apple juice (to retard oxidation of avocado)
½   cup diced fresh tomato
½   cup sour cream
1   teaspoon salt
    Pinch red pepper

In a food processor pulse the onion until finely chopped. Add the avocado and apple juice, and mix. Add the tomato, sour cream, salt, and pepper. Pulse until all is blended well.

THIS RECIPE	IS LOW IN HEME IRON AND CONTAINS
	substances that inhibit absorption of nonheme **IRON**
	calcium
X	dairy phosphate
	eggs
X	phytate phosphorus
	polyphenols tannic acid chlorogenic acid
X	phenolic acid
	oxalates

per serving IRON	heme iron MILLIGRAMS	nonheme iron MILLIGRAMS
	0.0	0.9

Barbecue Sauce

Makes 4½ to 5 cups; serving size: 2 tablespoons

4	tablespoons olive oil
1½	cups finely chopped onion
4	tablespoons minced garlic
1	6-ounce can tomato paste
3	cans hot strong black coffee
1	cup Heinz brand catsup
½	cup apple cider vinegar
1½	cups firmly packed brown sugar
4	tablespoons spicy mustard
½	teaspoon red pepper

IS LOW IN HEME IRON AND CONTAINS

THIS RECIPE	substances that inhibit absorption of nonheme IRON	
	calcium	
	dairy phosphate	
	eggs	
	phytate phosphorus	
	polyphenols tannic acid chlorogenic acid phenolic acid	X X
	oxalates	

In a stockpot heat the oil and sauté the onion and garlic until tender and golden, about 20 minutes.

Add the remaining ingredients and simmer for 1 hour.

Refrigerate and use as needed.

IRON	*per serving* heme iron MILLIGRAMS	nonheme iron MILLIGRAMS
	0.0	0.3

Brown Sauce

Makes 6 cups; serving size: ½ cup

½	cup olive oil
2	cups finely chopped onions
S	Salt and pepper to taste
½	cup flour
4	cups stock
1	cup brewed strong black coffee
1	stalk celery, chopped
1	parsnip, chopped
¼	cup tomato sauce
2	tablespoons chopped fresh parsley
1	tablespoon minced garlic
¼	teaspoon thyme
1	bay leaf

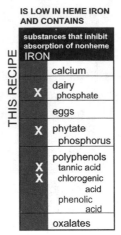

THIS RECIPE **IS LOW IN HEME IRON AND CONTAINS** substances that inhibit absorption of nonheme IRON

	calcium
X	dairy phosphate
	eggs
X	phytate phosphorus
X X	polyphenols tannic acid chlorogenic acid phenolic acid
	oxalates

In a skillet heat the oil and sauté the onion until tender and beginning to brown, about 20 minutes.

Season the onion with salt and pepper. Whisk the flour into the onion. Gently pour in the stock. Add the coffee, celery, parsnip, and tomato sauce. Add the parsley, garlic, thyme, and bay leaf. Simmer until reduced to a thick sauce.

Remove the bay leaf before serving.

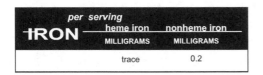

╂RON	per serving	
	heme iron MILLIGRAMS	nonheme iron MILLIGRAMS
	trace	0.2

Cheese Sauce
Serving size: ¼ cup

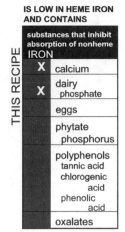

2	tablespoons olive oil (or butter)
4	tablespoons flour
1	teaspoon salt
¼	teaspoon white pepper
1¼	cups low fat milk

FOR BASIC AMERICAN MACARONI AND CHEESE SAUCE:

| ½ | cup cubed Velveeta cheese |
| ½ | cup shredded sharp Cheddar cheese |

FOR MORNAY:

| 1 | cup shredded Swiss cheese |

FOR ALFREDO:

| | Substitute cream for milk |
| 1 | cup grated Parmesan or Romano cheese |

In a skillet heat the oil. Whisk in the flour, salt, and pepper, and continue whisking until a paste forms. Very slowly add the milk, stirring until smooth. Season with salt and pepper. Blend in the cheeses as desired.

Other cheese choices include: mozzarella, havarti, fontina, Neufchatel, Monterey Jack, etc.

Note: Some cheeses melt better than others; combinations of cheeses can provide a better textured sauce.

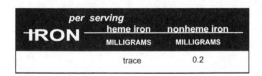

	per serving	
IRON	heme iron	nonheme iron
	MILLIGRAMS	MILLIGRAMS
	trace	0.2

Cream Sauce with Roasted Peppers

Makes 1½ cups; serving size: ¼ cup

1	**medium red bell pepper**
1	**cup milk**
2	**tablespoons olive oil**
4	**tablespoons flour**
1	**teaspoon salt**
¼	**teaspoon white pepper**
½	**cup heavy cream**

THIS RECIPE IS LOW IN HEME IRON AND CONTAINS

	substances that inhibit absorption of nonheme IRON
	calcium
X	dairy phosphate
	eggs
X	phytate phosphorus
	polyphenols tannic acid chlorogenic acid phenolic acid
	oxalates

Wash the pepper, remove the seeds and stem. Brush the pepper with olive oil and cut into slivers. Roast under the broiler for about 5 to 7 minutes.

Pour the milk into a food processor. Add the roasted peppers and blend. Prepare the roux: In a saucepan heat the olive oil. Blend in the flour until smooth. Slowly pour in the milk, blending until smooth. Season with salt and pepper. Add the heavy cream and reheat the sauce. It is delicious served over fish or vegetables.

IRON	*per serving*	
	heme iron MILLIGRAMS	nonheme iron MILLIGRAMS
	0.0	0.2

Chicken Velouté

Makes 2¼ cups or 6 servings

2	**tablespoons olive oil**
¼	**cup flour**
1	**teaspoon salt**
¼	**teaspoon white pepper**
½	**cup brewed coffee**
1½	**cups chicken broth**
¼	**cup finely diced chicken (white meat)**

In a skillet or saucepan heat the olive oil. Whisk in the flour, blending until smooth. Add salt and pepper, and stir until light brown. Slowly add the coffee and chicken broth. Add the chicken.

IS LOW IN HEME IRON AND CONTAINS

THIS RECIPE

substances that inhibit absorption of nonheme IRON	
	calcium
X	dairy phosphate
	eggs
X	phytate phosphorus
X X	polyphenols tannic acid chlorogenic acid phenolic acid
	oxalates

IRON	per serving	
	heme iron MILLIGRAMS	nonheme iron MILLIGRAMS
	0.03	0.4

Gravy

Makes 2¼ cups or 6 to 8 servings

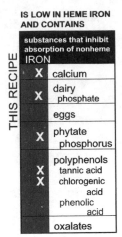

2	tablespoons olive oil	
¼	cup flour	
1	teaspoon salt	
¼	teaspoon black pepper	
1½	cups chicken or turkey broth	
½	cup coffee	
1	teaspoon instant coffee	

In a skillet or saucepan heat the oil. Whisk in the flour, blending until smooth. Add the salt and pepper. Slowly add the broth and coffee, blending well.

For white gravy omit the instant coffee and add ¼ cup of milk.

IRON	per serving	
	heme iron MILLIGRAMS	nonheme iron MILLIGRAMS
	0.26	0.5

IS LOW IN HEME IRON AND CONTAINS

THIS RECIPE

substances that inhibit absorption of nonheme IRON

X	calcium
X	dairy phosphate
	eggs
X	phytate phosphorus
X X	polyphenols tannic acid chlorogenic acid phenolic acid
	oxalates

Gumbo

Serves 6

¼	cup olive oil
2	cups chopped onion
1	cup diced celery, stems included
4	cups diced tomatoes
8	cups turkey or chicken broth
½	cup chopped fresh parsley
1	tablespoon instant coffee
2	bay leaves
1	tablespoon basil
1	tablespoon thyme
2	tablespoons minced garlic
1	tablespoon salt
	Red pepper to taste
¼	cup olive oil
½	cup flour

THIS RECIPE IS LOW IN HEME IRON AND CONTAINS

substances that inhibit absorption of nonheme IRON	
	calcium
X	dairy phosphate
	eggs
X	phytate phosphorus
X X	polyphenols tannic acid chlorogenic acid phenolic acid
	oxalates

In a skillet heat ¼ cup of olive oil and sauté the onion for about 20 minutes.

Add the celery and cook until tender. Add the tomatoes and cook an additional 20 minutes. Add the broth, parsley, instant coffee, bay leaves, basil, thyme, garlic, salt, and red pepper.

Prepare a roux: In a saucepan heat ¼ cup of olive oil. Add ½ cup of flour slowly, whisking into a paste. Continue cooking until the paste turns brown, but take care not to burn the roux. The next step is a bit tricky, so wear oven mitts to protect arms from splatter. Dip a cupful of liquid from the soup and add cautiously to the paste. Whisk constantly; continue to add cupfuls of soup to the paste until it is a gravy-like consistency. Whisk the gravy back into the soup. The soup will take on a cloudy appearance and will thicken slightly. Remove the bay leaves before serving.

Gumbo can be served over beans and rice and topped with chopped green onion.

IRON	per serving heme iron MILLIGRAMS	nonheme iron MILLIGRAMS
	trace	0.56

Marinara Sauce

Makes 8 cups; serving size: 1 cup

¼   cup olive oil

4   cups finely chopped onion

¼   cup minced garlic

1   14.5-ounce can diced tomatoes or 1 cup fresh

1   28-ounce can crushed tomatoes with purée

1   6-ounce can tomato paste

2   6-ounce cans hot coffee

1   cup chopped fresh parsley

1   teaspoon salt

    Red pepper to taste

IS LOW IN HEME IRON AND CONTAINS

THIS RECIPE

substances that inhibit absorption of nonheme IRON	
	calcium
X	dairy phosphate
	eggs
X	phytate phosphorus
X X	polyphenols tannic acid chlorogenic acid phenolic acid
	oxalates

In a saucepan heat the olive oil and sauté the onion and garlic for 20 minutes.

Add the diced tomatoes and simmer until the tomatoes are tender.

Add the tomato purée, tomato paste, and hot coffee. Add the parsley, and season with salt and pepper. Cover and simmer for 1 hour.

Uncover and simmer for 30 minutes.

Note: Due to the high beta-carotene content of this recipe, drinking tea is recommended.

IRON	per serving heme iron MILLIGRAMS	nonheme iron MILLIGRAMS
	0.0	0.58

Mushroom Velouté

Makes 4 cups; serving size: ¼ cup

2	tablespoons olive oil
¼	cup diced mushrooms
¼	cup oat flour
1	teaspoon salt
¼	teaspoon white pepper
1½	cups vegetable broth
½	cup brewed tea

In skillet or saucepan heat the olive oil and sauté the mushrooms until tender. Whisk in the flour, salt, and pepper. As the mixture turns brown, slowly add the broth and tea. Continue whisking until the mixture thickens.

THIS RECIPE IS LOW IN HEME IRON AND CONTAINS

	substances that inhibit absorption of nonheme IRON
	calcium
	dairy phosphate
	eggs
X	phytate phosphorus
X	polyphenols tannic acid chlorogenic acid phenolic acid
	oxalates

IRON	per serving heme iron MILLIGRAMS	nonheme iron MILLIGRAMS
	trace	0.28

Rosemary Sour Cream Sauce

Serves 4

2	tablespoons butter
2	tablespoons olive oil
2	tablespoons fresh or dried rosemary
2	tablespoons chives
1	cup sour cream

In a saucepan melt the butter. Add the oil, herbs, and sour cream. Whisk together and heat through but do not boil.

   Best served with potatoes, vegetables, or fish.

IS LOW IN HEME IRON AND CONTAINS

THIS RECIPE — substances that inhibit absorption of nonheme IRON

X	calcium
X	dairy phosphate
	eggs
	phytate phosphorus
	polyphenols tannic acid chlorogenic acid phenolic acid
X	oxalates

IRON	*per serving*	
	heme iron MILLIGRAMS	nonheme iron MILLIGRAMS
	trace	trace

Roux

2	tablespoons olive oil
4	tablespoons flour
1	teaspoon salt
1/8	teaspoon white pepper

In a glass skillet heat the oil. Whisk in the flour and continue whisking until a paste forms and begins to darken. Season with salt and pepper.

   From this roux the following recipes can be made: white sauce, cream sauce, gravy, cheese sauces, veloutés, and cream-based soups.

IRON	*per serving*	
	heme iron MILLIGRAMS	nonheme iron MILLIGRAMS
	trace	0.7

Sweet-and-Sour Sauce

Makes about 2 cups, serving size ¼ cup

1	tablespoon olive oil
1	cup green bell pepper cut into julienne strips
½	cup soy sauce
½	cup brown sugar
½	cup pineapple juice
½	teaspoon ground ginger root
1	tablespoon instant coffee
¼	cup water
2	teaspoons cornstarch

THIS RECIPE IS LOW IN HEME IRON AND CONTAINS

	substances that inhibit absorption of nonheme IRON
	calcium
X	dairy phosphate
	eggs
X	phytate phosphorus
X X	polyphenols tannic acid chlorogenic acid phenolic acid
	oxalates

In a saucepan heat the oil and sauté the peppers until tender. Remove from the skillet and set aside.

In the same skillet combine the soy sauce, brown sugar, pineapple juice, ginger root, and coffee, and bring to a boil.

In a shaker container mix the water and cornstarch; shake vigorously. Using a whisk, stir the sauce briskly and add the cornstarch-water mixture to the boiling sauce whisking constantly. The sauce should thicken slightly.

IRON	per serving heme iron MILLIGRAMS	nonheme iron MILLIGRAMS
	trace	1.0

Vegetable Velouté

Makes 2¼ cups or 6 servings

2	tablespoons olive oil
¼	cup finely diced vegetable of choice: celery, onion or leeks, parsnips, spinach, kale, carrot, red, green, or yellow peppers
¼	cup flour
1	teaspoon salt
¼	teaspoon white pepper
1½	cups vegetable broth
½	cup brewed tea

THIS RECIPE	IS LOW IN HEME IRON AND CONTAINS	
	substances that inhibit absorption of nonheme IRON	
		calcium
	X	dairy phosphate
		eggs
	X	phytate phosphorus
	X	polyphenols tannic acid chlorogenic acid phenolic acid
	X	oxalates

In skillet or saucepan heat the olive oil. Add the desired vegetable and sauté until tender. Whisk in the flour. Season with salt and pepper. Stir until light brown. Slowly add the broth and tea, and blend until smooth.

IRON	per serving	
	heme iron MILLIGRAMS	nonheme iron MILLIGRAMS
	0.0	0.4

White Sauce

Makes 1½ cups; serving size: ¼ cup

2	tablespoons olive oil
4	tablespoons flour
1	teaspoon salt
¼	teaspoon white pepper
1¼	cups low fat milk

THIS RECIPE	IS LOW IN HEME IRON AND CONTAINS	
	substances that inhibit absorption of nonheme IRON	
		calcium
	X	dairy phosphate
		eggs
	X	phytate phosphorus
		polyphenols tannic acid chlorogenic acid phenolic acid
		oxalates

In a saucepan heat the olive oil and blend in the flour. Season with salt and pepper. Very slowly add the milk, blending well.

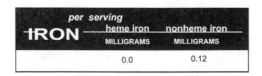

IRON	per serving	
	heme iron MILLIGRAMS	nonheme iron MILLIGRAMS
	0.0	0.12

Apple Oatmeal Cookies
Makes 2 dozen

1	cup chopped seeded apples
2	tablespoons apple juice
½	cup butter
⅔	cup light brown sugar
2	eggs
1	cup oat blend flour
1	teaspoon baking powder
1	teaspoon cinnamon
½	teaspoon nutmeg
½	teaspoon salt
1	cup oats
1	cup English walnuts

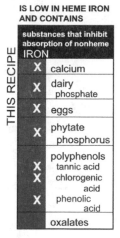

IS LOW IN HEME IRON AND CONTAINS

THIS RECIPE	substances that inhibit absorption of nonheme IRON	
	X	calcium
	X	dairy phosphate
	X	eggs
	X	phytate phosphorus
	X	polyphenols tannic acid
	X	chlorogenic acid
	X	phenolic acid
		oxalates

In a food processor place the apples and apple juice, and pulse until the apples are coarse chunks.

In a separate bowl cream the butter and sugar. Add the eggs and blend well. Sift the flour, baking powder, cinnamon, nutmeg, and salt into the mixture. Stir in the oats and apples, and mix well. Fold in the nuts. Spoon onto a greased baking sheet. Bake at 350° for 10 to 15 minutes.

IRON	per serving heme iron MILLIGRAMS	nonheme iron MILLIGRAMS
	0.0	0.2

Baked Dutch Apple Pie
Serves 8

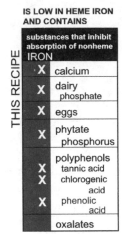

		IS LOW IN HEME IRON AND CONTAINS
		substances that inhibit absorption of nonheme IRON
	X	calcium
	X	dairy phosphate
	X	eggs
	X	phytate phosphorus
	X X	polyphenols tannic acid chlorogenic acid
	X	phenolic acid
		oxalates

(left column label: THIS RECIPE)

8	peeled, seeded, and sliced cooking apples
1½	tablespoons apple juice
⅔	cup light brown sugar, firmly packed
¼	teaspoon salt
¼	cup oat blend flour
1	teaspoon ground cinnamon
1	tablespoon instant tea
½	teaspoon ground nutmeg
1	9-inch pie crust

TOPPING:

1	cup flour
⅔	cup firmly packed light brown sugar
½	cup butter, melted

Preheat the oven to 350°.

In a large bowl combine the apples, apple juice, ⅔ cup of brown sugar, salt, ¼ cup of flour, cinnamon, instant tea, and nutmeg. Mix the ingredients well, then spoon into the crust.

Prepare the topping: In a separate bowl combine with a fork 1 cup of flour, ⅔ cup of brown sugar, and ½ cup of butter. Sprinkle the topping mixture evenly over the apples. Place the pie on a baking sheet and bake for about 55 to 60 minutes until the topping is golden and the filling bubbles.

IRON	per serving	
	heme iron MILLIGRAMS	nonheme iron MILLIGRAMS
	0.0	1.1

Banana Pudding

1	12-ounce box vanilla wafers
4	large bananas
2½	cups cold milk
½	cup chilled tea
1	4-ounce package Jello-O brand instant vanilla pudding mix
	Whipped topping of your choice

In a large bowl alternate layers of vanilla wafers and sliced bananas.

In a separate bowl mix the milk, tea, and pudding with a wire whisk. Work quickly so the mixture does not thicken before pouring over the bananas. Top with whipped cream or nondairy topping.

IS LOW IN HEME IRON AND CONTAINS

THIS RECIPE

	substances that inhibit absorption of nonheme IRON
X	calcium
X	dairy phosphate
	eggs
X	phytate phosphorus
X X	polyphenols tannic acid chlorogenic acid phenolic acid
	oxalates

IRON	per serving	
	heme iron MILLIGRAMS	nonheme iron MILLIGRAMS
	0.0	0.5

Buttermilk Sheetcake
Serves 12

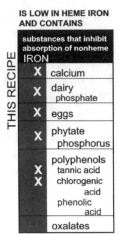

¾   cup butter

2   cups light brown sugar

2   eggs

1   teaspoon vanilla extract

1   teaspoon baking soda

1¼   cups buttermilk

2¾   cups flour

1   teaspoon baking powder

¼   teaspoon salt

1   heaping teaspoon cinnamon

TOPPING:

2   egg whites

1   cup light brown sugar

½   cup walnuts

In a large bowl cream the butter and 2 cups of brown sugar together. Add the 2 eggs and beat well. Add the vanilla.

Sprinkle the baking soda into the buttermilk and set aside.

In a separate bowl mix the flour, baking powder, salt, and cinnamon. Alternate adding the dry ingredients and buttermilk to the creamed mixture. stirring with a wooden spoon.

Oil and flour a 9 x 13-inch baking dish. Pour the cake batter into the dish.

Prepare the topping: In the bowl of an electric mixer beat 2 egg whites until soft peaks form. Slowly fold the whites into 1 cup of light brown sugar. Add the English walnuts. Spoon evenly over the cake batter. Bake at 325° for 40 minutes.

IRON	*per serving*	
	heme iron MILLIGRAMS	nonheme iron MILLIGRAMS
	0.0	1.3

Chess Pie

Serves 8

2	cups firmly packed light brown sugar
1	tablespoon oat blend flour
1	tablespoon Yelton's brand cornmeal
1	teaspoon cinnamon
¼	teaspoon salt
¼	cup olive oil
½	cup apple juice
½	cup light cream
1	teaspoon instant tea
4	eggs, lightly beaten
1	9-inch unbaked pie shell

THIS RECIPE	IS LOW IN HEME IRON AND CONTAINS	
	substances that inhibit absorption of nonheme IRON	
	X	calcium
	X	dairy phosphate
	X	eggs
	X	phytate phosphorus
	X X	polyphenols tannic acid chlorogenic acid phenolic acid
		oxalates

In a large bowl mix the sugar, flour, cornmeal, cinnamon, and salt. Add the oil, juice, cream, and tea, and blend well. Add the eggs and blend well. Pour the mixture into the unbaked pie shell. Bake at 350° for 40 minutes.

IRON	per serving heme iron MILLIGRAMS	nonheme iron MILLIGRAMS
	0.0	1.36

Coffee Liqueur Chocolate Cake
Serves 8

1	18¼-ounce box Duncan Hines devil's food cake mix
1	4-ounce package Jell-O brand instant chocolate pudding
½	cup strong coffee
½	cup Faux Molasses (see recipe on page 216)
1	cup buttermilk
¼	teaspoon baking soda
½	cup olive oil
4	eggs
1	6-ounce bag semisweet chocolate bits

IS LOW IN HEME IRON
AND CONTAINS

THIS RECIPE	substances that inhibit absorption of nonheme IRON	
	X	calcium
	X	dairy phosphate
	X	eggs
	X	phytate phosphorus
	X X	polyphenols tannic acid chlorogenic acid phenolic acid
		oxalates

Spray the inside of a bundt cake pan generously with vegetable spray.

In a large bowl blend all of the ingredients, folding in the chocolate chips last. Pour the batter evenly into the prepared bundt pan. Bake at 350° for 40 minutes.

+IRON	per serving	
	heme iron MILLIGRAMS	nonheme iron MILLIGRAMS
	0.0	0.47

Custard Apple Pie

Serves 8

1	9-inch pie crust
3	cups peeled, seeded, and diced Granny Smith apples
2	tablespoons apple juice (to retard discoloration)
2	tablespoons olive oil
1	teaspoon cinnamon
1	egg
1	14-ounce can sweetened condensed milk

THIS RECIPE IS LOW IN HEME IRON AND CONTAINS

	substances that inhibit absorption of nonheme IRON
X	calcium
X	dairy phosphate
X	eggs
X	phytate phosphorus
X	polyphenols tannic acid
X	chlorogenic acid
X	phenolic acid
	oxalates

Preheat the oven to 375°. Bake the pie crust for 5 to 7 minutes until light brown.

In a saucepan simmer the apples, apple juice, oil, and cinnamon on low heat until the apples are tender and the liquid evaporates. Mash the cooked apples into coarse applesauce and pour into the baked pie crust. In a medium bowl beat the egg into the condensed milk. Pour over the apples. Bake at 350° for 40 minutes.

IRON	per serving	
	heme iron MILLIGRAMS	nonheme iron MILLIGRAMS
	0.0	0.25

Faux Molasses

Makes 1½ cups

	substances that inhibit absorption of nonheme IRON
X	calcium
	dairy phosphate
	eggs
	phytate phosphorus
X X	polyphenols tannic acid chlorogenic acid phenolic acid
	oxalates

THIS RECIPE

2   **cups firmly packed brown sugar**

1   **cup water**

2   **tablespoons instant decaffeinated coffee**

In a saucepan combine all of the ingredients. Bring to a boil. Allow to boil for 5 minutes.

Remove the pan from the heat and let stand until thickened.

IRON	per serving	
	heme iron	nonheme iron
	MILLIGRAMS	MILLIGRAMS
	0.0	1.4

Ice Cream Cake
Serves 8 to 10

	IS LOW IN HEME IRON AND CONTAINS

Prepare 1 chocolate brownie recipe in one 9-inch round cake pan.

Let ½ gallon Breyer's brand coffee ice cream soften for 30 minutes or longer to thaw slightly.

Empty the ice cream into a 9-inch cake pan and press firmly, distributing the ice cream evenly. Refreeze overnight.

Thaw 1 tub of whipped topping overnight.

To assemble: Place the baked and cooled brownie on a flat dinner plate. Fill the kitchen sink with 4 to 6 inches of warm water. Holding the cake pan with frozen ice cream, carefully submerge the pan up to the rim in the warm water. Take care not to allow the water to splash onto the ice cream. Gently move the pan back and forth until the frozen contents loosen. Place the cake layer on top of the frozen ice cream. Secure the cake with one hand and the ice cream pan with the other hand. Flip both the cake and pan over so the cake is on the bottom and the pan can be removed from the ice cream layer now on top. Slide the cake onto a flat dish. Place the cake in the freezer for 1 hour.

Frost the cake with whipped topping.

Tip: Frozen yogurt or ice milk can be substituted.

THIS RECIPE

	substances that inhibit absorption of nonheme IRON
X	calcium
X	dairy phosphate
X	eggs
X	phytate phosphorus
X X	polyphenols tannic acid chlorogenic acid phenolic acid
	oxalates

IRON	per serving heme iron MILLIGRAMS	nonheme iron MILLIGRAMS
	0.0	0.7

Lime Jell-O Salad

Serves 8

1	cup hot tea
1	6-ounce box lime Jell-O
1	8-ounce package Neufchatel cream cheese
1	cup cold apple juice
½	cup chopped apples
¼	cup chopped celery
½	cup chopped English walnuts
	Sour cream for topping

THIS RECIPE

IS LOW IN HEME IRON AND CONTAINS substances that inhibit absorption of nonheme IRON

X	calcium
X	dairy phosphate
	eggs
X	phytate phosphorus
X X	polyphenols tannic acid chlorogenic acid phenolic acid
	oxalates

In a large bowl pour the hot tea over the gelatin and stir until completely dissolved. Add the Neufchatel and mix until the cheese is blended. Add the cold apple juice, apples, celery, and nuts. Stir and pour into a sprayed mold or glass dish. Refrigerate until set.

Serve with a dollop of sour cream.

IRON	per serving heme iron MILLIGRAMS	nonheme iron MILLIGRAMS
	0.0	0.3

Mocha Almond Biscotti

Makes 18

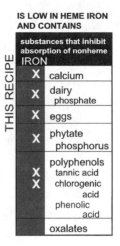

IS LOW IN HEME IRON
AND CONTAINS

THIS RECIPE	substances that inhibit absorption of nonheme IRON	
	X	calcium
	X	dairy phosphate
	X	eggs
	X	phytate phosphorus
	X X	polyphenols tannic acid chlorogenic acid phenolic acid
		oxalates

2½ cups raw almonds

3 cups oat blend flour

¼ cup cocoa

1 tablespoon instant coffee

2½ teaspoons baking powder

¼ teaspoon salt

½ cup butter

1 cup sugar

3 eggs

1 teaspoon vanilla extract

1 teaspoon almond extract

Place the raw almonds on a cookie sheet and roast at 425° for 15 minutes. Remove from the oven and let stand 20 minutes or until crunchy. Chop in a food processor.

In a medium bowl combine the flour, cocoa, instant coffee, baking powder, and salt.

In the bowl of an electric mixer cream the butter and sugar together. Add the eggs and continue to beat at medium speed. Add the dry ingredients. Blend in the vanilla and almond extracts and the nuts. Blend well, the dough will be stiff. Turn dough out onto a floured pastry cloth. Form into 2 long oval-shaped flattened logs. Place on a cookie sheet. Bake at 350° for about 20 minutes.

Transfer to a cool surface and cut the logs widthwise into 1½-inch-wide pieces. Place the pieces on their sides on the cookie sheet and bake at 400° for 10 minutes.

Remove and cool before eating

IRON	per serving	
	heme iron MILLIGRAMS	nonheme iron MILLIGRAMS
	trace	0.95

Mocha Angel Food

Serves 8

1¼	cups sifted cake flour
2	tablespoons instant coffee
3	tablespoons cocoa
12	large egg whites (let stand to reach room temperature)
1½	teaspoons cream of tartar
¼	teaspoon salt
1	cup sugar
1	teaspoon vanilla extract

THIS RECIPE	IS LOW IN HEME IRON AND CONTAINS	
	substances that inhibit absorption of nonheme IRON	
	X	calcium
	X	dairy phosphate
	X	eggs
	X	phytate phosphorus
	X X	polyphenols tannic acid chlorogenic acid phenolic acid
		oxalates

Place the oven rack on the lowest level and preheat the oven to 350°.

In a medium bowl sift the flour, coffee, and cocoa powder together 4 times and set aside.

In the bowl of an electric mixer beat the egg whites until foamy. Add the cream of tartar and salt. Turn the mixer to low speed and alternately add the sugar and flour mixture in small amounts to the whipped egg white mixture. Drizzle in the vanilla. Pour into a nonstick angel food cake pan. Bake at 350° for 40 to 45 minutes or until the cake springs back upon touch.

Invert the pan onto a cooling rack and let stand to cool.

CHOCOLATE-COFFEE SAUCE (Optional, not recommended for diabetics):

¾	cup sweetened condensed milk
½	cup semisweet chocolate bits
2	tablespoons instant coffee

In a medium saucepan heat the condensed milk. Add the chocolate bits and coffee, and whip with a whisk until smooth and creamy. While warm, drizzle over the top of the cake.

IRON	per serving	
	heme iron MILLIGRAMS	nonheme iron MILLIGRAMS
	0.0	0.7

Mocha Cheesecake
Serves 12

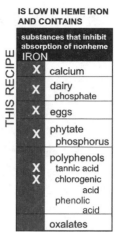

**IS LOW IN HEME IRON
AND CONTAINS**

THIS RECIPE	substances that inhibit absorption of nonheme IRON	
	X	calcium
	X	dairy phosphate
	X	eggs
	X	phytate phosphorus
	X X	polyphenols tannic acid chlorogenic acid phenolic acid
		oxalates

CRUST:

1½	cups graham cracker crumbs
⅓	cup brown sugar
⅓	cup olive oil

FILLING:

4	8-ounce packages cream cheese
1	cup sugar
3	tablespoons flour
½	cup Hershey's brand cocoa
1	tablespoon instant coffee
1¼	cups sour cream
2	teaspoons vanilla extract
4	eggs

TOPPING:

½	cup sour cream
1	tablespoon milk
	Cocoa powder for garnish

In a medium bowl blend together the graham cracker crumbs, brown sugar, and olive oil. Press into the bottom of a 10-inch springform pan.

In the bowl of an electric mixer combine the cream cheese, sugar, flour, cocoa, and coffee. Beat until fluffy. Add the sour cream and vanilla, then eggs one at a time. Blend well on low speed. Pour into the graham cracker crust. Bake at 300° for 1 hour. Cool.

In a small bowl combine the sour cream and milk. Pour over the top of the cheesecake. Cool the cheesecake in the refrigerator overnight, or at least 6 hours before removing the outside ring.

Slide a thin-blade knife between the cheesecake and the bottom of the pan. Slip the cheesecake onto a glass plate. Garnish with sprinkle of cocoa powder.

IRON	*per serving* heme iron MILLIGRAMS	nonheme iron MILLIGRAMS
	0.0	0.9

Mocha Cream Pie

Serves 6

½	cup sugar
5	egg yolks
1	cup milk
3	ounces semisweet chocolate
1	ounce unsweetened chocolate
1	tablespoon instant coffee
1½	packets unflavored gelatin
1	tablespoon cold coffee
1	cup heavy cream
1	9-inch pie shell, baked

THIS RECIPE

IS LOW IN HEME IRON AND CONTAINS

	substances that inhibit absorption of nonheme IRON
X	calcium
X	dairy phosphate
X	eggs
X	phytate phosphorus
X X	polyphenols tannic acid chlorogenic acid phenolic acid
	oxalates

In the bowl of an electric mixer combine the sugar and egg yolks. Beat on high until the mixture is pale lemon-colored.

In a saucepan heat the milk on medium low. Add the chocolate squares and instant coffee and stir until melted and smooth.

In a separate bowl dissolve the gelatin with cold coffee. Blend the gelatin into the warm milk-chocolate mixture and stir with a wooden spoon for about 5 to 7 minutes. Begin adding the egg-sugar mixture to the chocolate mixture. Stir quickly so the egg does not cook. Once blended, pour the mixture into a large bowl and set the bottom of the bowl into an ice water bath. Stir until the mixture thickens. Whip the cream until soft peaks form. Fold into the chocolate pudding. Blend thoroughly. Pour into the baked pie crust. Refrigerate.

IRON	*per serving*	
	heme iron	nonheme iron
	MILLIGRAMS	MILLIGRAMS
	0.0	1.0

Mocha Nut Triangles

Makes 1 pound

2¼ cups ground English walnuts
2 cups confectioners' sugar
2 tablespoons Folger's brand instant decaf coffee
2 tablespoons brewed hot decaf coffee
½ cup semisweet chocolate bits

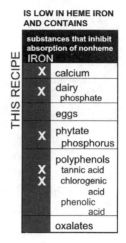

THIS RECIPE	IS LOW IN HEME IRON AND CONTAINS	
	substances that inhibit absorption of nonheme IRON	
	X	calcium
	X	dairy phosphate
		eggs
	X	phytate phosphorus
	X X	polyphenols tannic acid chlorogenic acid phenolic acid
		oxalates

In a medium bowl combine 2 cups of nuts and 1¾ cups of the confectioners' sugar. Stir in 1 tablespoon of instant coffee and add 1 tablespoon of the hot brewed coffee. Work the mixture into a ball and refrigerate overnight.

Sift confectioners' sugar onto the surface of the ball and roll out on a clean flat surface. Cut into wide strips, and score each strip to create rectangles. Cut each rectangle on the diagonal to create triangles.

In the top of a double boiler over simmering water melt the chocolate bits. Add ¼ cup of confectioners' sugar. Add the remaining 1 tablespoon of instant coffee and 1 tablespoon of brewed coffee, and stir until the chocolate is silky. Spoon the chocolate over the triangles. Decorate with a pinch of ground nuts.

IRON	*per serving*	
	heme iron MILLIGRAMS	nonheme iron MILLIGRAMS
	0.0	0.8

Mocha Tiramisu

Serves 12

12	ladyfingers
3	cups milk
⅔	cup sugar
¼	teaspoon salt
2	tablespoons instant coffee granules
2	packets unflavored gelatin
¼	cup brewed cold coffee
¼	cup Faux Molasses (see recipe on page 216)
2	cups heavy cream

THIS RECIPE

IS LOW IN HEME IRON AND CONTAINS

substances that inhibit absorption of nonheme IRON	
X	calcium
X	dairy phosphate
	eggs
X	phytate phosphorus
X X	polyphenols tannic acid chlorogenic acid phenolic acid
	oxalates

Line the sides of a large straight glass bowl with ladyfingers.

In a glass saucepan heat the milk over medium-low heat. Add the sugar, salt, and instant coffee granules to the warm milk. In a separate bowl dissolve the gelatin in cold coffee. When dissolved, add the gelatin mixture to the warm milk mixture and stir with a wooden spoon for about 5 to 7 minutes until the pudding thickens. Add the Faux Molasses to the pudding and chill slightly.

In the bowl of an electric mixer whip the cream until soft peaks form. Fold into the pudding. Pour the mixture into the center of the ladyfinger-lined bowl. Refrigerate.

IRON	per serving heme iron MILLIGRAMS	nonheme iron MILLIGRAMS
	0.0	trace

Peanut Butter Cookies

Makes 24 cookies

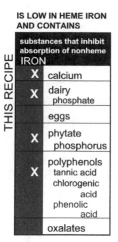

1	cup sugar
1	cup firmly packed light brown sugar
½	cup olive oil
1	cup Jif brand chunky peanut butter
2	eggs
1	teaspoon vanilla extract
2½	to 3 cups flour
1	teaspoon baking soda
1	teaspoon salt

In a large bowl cream together the sugars, oil, and peanut butter. Add the eggs and vanilla.

In a separate bowl sift together the flour, baking soda, and salt. Add slowly to the sugar mixture. The dough will be stiff as the flour is worked into it. When all sides of the bowl are clean, using an ice cream scoop with a release handle, scoop the dough onto a lightly oiled cookie sheet. Mash each cookie and make a criss-cross design on top using the tines of a dinner fork. Bake at 350° for 6 to 8 minutes or until brown around the edges.

IRON	per serving heme iron MILLIGRAMS	nonheme iron MILLIGRAMS
	0.0	0.5

Peanut Butter Chocolate Ice Cream Pie
Serves 8

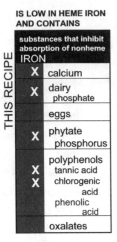

1	8-ounce package Neufchatel cheese
1¼	cups confectioners' sugar
1	cup crunchy Jif brand peanut butter
2	cups light cream
2	tablespoons Hershey's cocoa
1	9-inch pie shell, baked
¼	cup chopped peanuts

In a large bowl combine the cream cheese, sugar, cocoa, and peanut butter.

In the bowl of an electric mixer whip the cream until soft peaks form. Fold the whipped cream into the peanut butter mixture. Pour the filling into the pie crust. Sprinkle chopped nuts over the surface. Place the pie in the freezer overnight. Allow the pie to soften slightly (about 20 minutes) before serving.

IRON	*per serving*	
	heme iron	nonheme iron
	MILLIGRAMS	MILLIGRAMS
	0.0	0.8

Pie Crust

Makes two 9-inch pie crusts

2	**cups flour**
1	**teaspoon salt**
½	**pound Crisco shortening**
4	**to 5 tablespoons cold skim milk**

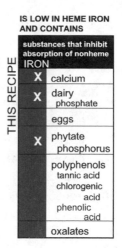

Place the flour and salt in a food processor. Pinch the shortening into pieces and drop into the flour. Pulse until blended. Gently add the cold milk a bit at a time, and pulse. Do not overprocess; the dough should stick together but should not be gooey. Remove and form into a smooth ball.

Tip: Wrap in waxed paper and refrigerate for 1 hour. The dough will be easier to handle.

Flour a pastry cloth. Separate the dough ball into 2 pieces, roll out, and line the baking dish with one crust. Use the second for the cover or refrigerate for another use.

IRON	per serving	
	heme iron	nonheme iron
	MILLIGRAMS	MILLIGRAMS
	0.0	1.17

Plum Cake
Serves 8

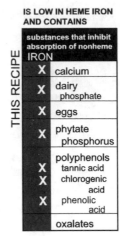

2	cups whole-wheat flour
1	cup cocoa powder
1	teaspoon baking powder
2	teaspoons baking soda
¼	teaspoon salt
1⅔	cups sugar
10	ounces puréed plums
2	teaspoons vanilla extract
2	eggs
1	cup buttermilk
1	cup hot strong coffee
1	tablespoon instant coffee

GLAZE:

2	cups confectioners' sugar
¼	cup butter, melted
⅓	cup strong coffee

In a medium bowl sift the flour, cocoa, baking powder, baking soda, and salt together.

In a large bowl blend the sugar, puréed plums, vanilla, and eggs. Alternately add the flour mixture and the buttermilk and coffee. Stir the batter until blended.

Spray a rectangular baking dish generously with vegetable spray. Pour the batter into the prepared dish. Bake at 350° for 30 to 35 minutes until the center is done.

While still hot, poke holes in the cake. In a medium bowl combine the glaze ingredients and blend well. Pour the mixture over the surface of the cake and let cool.

IS LOW IN HEME IRON AND CONTAINS

THIS RECIPE

	substances that inhibit absorption of nonheme IRON
X	calcium
X	dairy phosphate
X	eggs
X	phytate phosphorus
X X	polyphenols tannic acid chlorogenic acid
X	phenolic acid
	oxalates

IRON — per serving

	heme iron MILLIGRAMS	nonheme iron MILLIGRAMS
	0.0	1.36

Raspberry Squares
Makes 24

3	cups oat blend flour
2	teaspoon baking powder
1	teaspoon salt
1	tablespoon instant tea
3	teaspoons sugar
1	cup (2 sticks) butter
½	cup olive oil
1	egg
⅔	cup raspberry jam
1	cup ground English walnuts

IS LOW IN HEME IRON AND CONTAINS

THIS RECIPE

	substances that inhibit absorption of nonheme IRON
X	calcium
X	dairy phosphate
X	eggs
X	phytate phosphorus
X	polyphenols tannic acid
X	chlorogenic acid
X	phenolic acid
	oxalates

In a large bowl combine the flour, baking powder, salt, tea, and sugar. Cut in the butter with a fork or pastry cutter. Add the lightly beaten egg and the oil. The dough will be very stiff. Roll the dough into a rectangle ¼ inch thick.

Spray a cookie sheet with vegetable spray. Place the dough on cookie sheet and press the edges out so the dough covers the cookie sheet. Spread raspberry jam over the surface of the dough and sprinkle with ground nuts. Before baking, score the dough into 24 cookies using a pizza cutter. Bake at 350° for 12 to 15 minutes until the cookie is done.

Let stand 15 minutes before snapping the cookies apart.

IRON	per serving	
	heme iron MILLIGRAMS	nonheme iron MILLIGRAMS
	0.0	0.8

Spiced Apple Dessert Casserole
Serves 8

¼   cup olive oil
3   cups whole-wheat bread crumbs
4   cups diced apples
¼   cup apple juice
½   cup orange juice
¼   cup sugar
¼   teaspoon salt
½   teaspoon ground cloves
¼   cup dry white wine

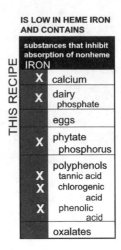

IS LOW IN HEME IRON AND CONTAINS

THIS RECIPE	substances that inhibit absorption of nonheme IRON	
	X	calcium
	X	dairy phosphate
		eggs
	X	phytate phosphorus
	X	polyphenols tannic acid
	X	chlorogenic acid
	X	phenolic acid
		oxalates

In a medium bowl combine the olive oil and bread crumbs. Set aside.

In a separate bowl mix the apples, juices, sugar, salt, cloves, and wine. Alternate layers of bread crumbs and apple mixture in an oiled 1-quart glass dish. Cover and bake at 350°. Uncover and bake an additional 15 to 20 minutes.

IRON	per serving heme iron MILLIGRAMS	nonheme iron MILLIGRAMS
	0.0	0.8

Strawberry Jell-O Salad

Serves 8

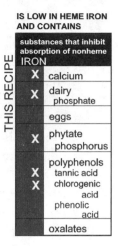

	IS LOW IN HEME IRON AND CONTAINS
	substances that inhibit absorption of nonheme
THIS RECIPE	IRON
X	calcium
X	dairy phosphate
	eggs
X	phytate phosphorus
X	polyphenols tannic acid
X	chlorogenic acid
	phenolic acid
	oxalates

1	cup hot green tea
1	6-ounce package strawberry Jell-O mix
1	10-ounce box frozen strawberries with liquid
1	6-ounce can crushed pineapple, drained
1	8-ounce package Neufchatel cheese
½	cup cold apple juice
½	cup chopped English walnuts
¼	cup sour cream
1	tablespoon milk

Pour boiling hot tea over the gelatin and stir until the gelatin is dissolved. Add the frozen strawberries and pineapple.

Place the cream cheese in a food processor. Add the apple juice and pulse until runny. Add to the gelatin and fruit mixture. Fold in the nuts. Chill until set.

In a small bowl combine the sour cream and milk. Pour over the top of the set gelatin.

IRON	per serving	
	heme iron	nonheme iron
	MILLIGRAMS	MILLIGRAMS
	0.0	0.7

Strawberries and Cream Cake

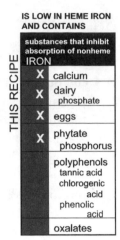

1½   cups fresh Driscoll brand strawberries
1   3.4-ounce box Jell-O brand instant vanilla pudding
1½   cups cold milk
½   cup cold green tea
1   18¼-ounce box Duncan Hines brand yellow cake mix
1   pint heavy cream or nondairy topping

Wash the strawberries and pat dry. Slice and stir into the pudding; reserve a few strawberries for garnish.

In a medium bowl combine the instant pudding, milk, and tea and mix as directed on the package. Chill until set.

Bake the yellow cake according to the instructions for 2 layers. Cool and split the layers. Spread a generous portion of pudding between the split layers but not on top.

In the bowl of an electric mixer whip the cream until stiff peaks form. Spread the cake with whipped topping. Refrigerate until served.

Note: Because strawberries are high in vitamin C, this dessert is best consumed 2 hours after a meal and with coffee.

＋RON	*per serving*	
	heme iron	nonheme iron
	MILLIGRAMS	MILLIGRAMS
	0.0	0.9

Sugar Cream Pie
Serves 8

½	**cup butter**
1	**cup sugar**
2	**cups light cream**
¼	**cup cornstarch**
¼	**cup milk**
1	**9-inch pie shell, baked**
¼	**teaspoon nutmeg**

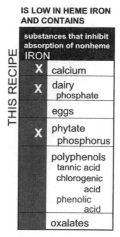

THIS RECIPE **IS LOW IN HEME IRON AND CONTAINS** substances that inhibit absorption of nonheme IRON

X	calcium
X	dairy phosphate
	eggs
X	phytate phosphorus
	polyphenols tannic acid chlorogenic acid phenolic acid
	oxalates

In the top of a double boiler heat the butter, sugar, and cream until hot but not boiling.

In a container with a lid mix the cornstarch with the milk and shake vigorously. Pour into the butter mixture, stir, and continue cooking for 5 minutes. Pour the filling into the baked shell. Sprinkle nutmeg over the surface. Bake at 400° for 5 to 6 minutes.

Refrigerate and serve chilled.

IRON	per serving heme iron MILLIGRAMS	nonheme iron MILLIGRAMS
	0.0	trace

Personal Stories

Diet Success Stories from People Living with Hemochromatosis

Susan's story: "I was diagnosed in my thirties with hemochromatosis. My ferritin was only around 400 even though I had many symptoms. I only weighed around 100 pounds and my treatment went very slow. Doctors soon realized they had to increase the volume of blood removed slowly. They found that they could only take one half pint of blood every other week, then one half pint weekly. This was all my body would allow. Still, I hardly made any headway with my (iron) levels. One day while I was expressing my frustration to Chris Kieffer at Iron Disorders Institute, she asked about my diet. When I told her that I was a big beef-eater she offered some diet suggestions that included cutting back on red meat and drinking tea with my meals. We concluded that with all the beef I was eating, I was apparently absorbing about the same amount of iron that was being removed. When I made these simple changes in my diet, which reduced my iron intake and helped to block what iron I did consume, my iron levels started dropping significantly. After I was diagnosed my husband had begun to develop symptoms similar to mine. I urged him to get tested for hemochromatosis, which he did and it was found that he, too, had the disorder. A book like *Cooking with Less Iron* would have been a tremendous help to understand hemochromatosis and the effect diet plays, especially on treatment. For sure, a meal plan would have made things simpler especially since we were both in treatment at the same time."

Harry's story: "I was diagnosed with hemochromatosis at age forty-nine with a very high ferritin of 2,960 and a saturation of 98 percent. I was especially careful with my iron intake during the deironing phase. It seemed logical that if I needed to remove iron then I should take in less iron so as not to prolong my treatments. My wife had read a lot about iron and adjusted our diets, including eliminating spinach and other high-iron foods. After calling a scientist at NIH (National Institutes of Health) we started eating vegetables again that contained iron. The scientist explained that vegetable and fruit sources of iron were not as readily available to the body as beef. The scientist also told my wife that I should eat a balanced diet. We reduced our red meat intake tremendously . . . that was good (because that was the biggest source of iron to the body). We had already changed cereal from our favorite of Special K to a low fortified one and avoided orange juice with breakfast. Our stress-formula daily vitamin with extra iron was a very bad choice. For the previous seven years, we had thought we were being good to ourselves by taking this daily vitamin, but we had in fact compounded my problems. My wife then called a scientist with Tetley Tea, who confirmed that the tannins in tea blocked iron absorption. She questioned if the decaffienating process also might remove the valuable tannins. She was told it did not! So we increased tea consumption. I also traveled a lot and enjoyed raw oysters. Looking back at my very high iron levels I guess I am lucky to be alive with the bacteria raw oysters sometimes contain; what I was eating could have killed me. When I was diagnosed nine years ago we could find very little information about this iron loading disorder, especially about diet. We didn't have a computer and knew little of the Internet. A book like this one would have made life easier."

Art's story: Art set off metal detectors in airports for years before he was diagnosed with an inherited iron loading condition called G6PD deficiency. Glucose 6 phosphate dehydrogenase (G6PD) is an enzyme deficiency more prevalent in males than females. It is one of several anemias where iron overload can be a consequence. Persons with G6PD are prone to hemolysis (red blood cell destruction), which leads to iron overload. Once diagnosed, Art found that certain antibiotics, sinus medication, and alcohol made his condition flare up. He was also told that eating fava beans could trigger an episode of hemolysis. Art's serum ferritin at time of diagnosis was over 1,500 with an accompanying saturation percentage of 70 percent. He began treatment but after removal of 20 pints of blood, his ferritin level only dropped to 1,390 and his saturation percentage remained well above 50 percent. Art decided that diet changes must be made. He decided to stick to a low-iron diet and to make every effort to limit the amount of iron absorbed. Art says, "I consider my G6PD hemolytic anemia much different and more complex than hemochromatosis. Iron disorder treatments are similar but phlebotomy rates and frequency and iron absorption rates differ with each individual. Some people may not think diet is important. I had a physician tell me that diet wouldn't matter in my case, but I have learned that diet is a big deal. I believe a low-iron diet has to be adhered to in my case. I think a book like *Cooking with Less Iron* can be helpful for anyone at risk for iron overload."

David's story: "I have an iron loading disorder but doctors can't figure out why I absorb extra iron, because I don't have the typical gene mutations for hemochromatosis. Also my iron loading condition showed up when I was only sixteen, which is unusual for people with HHC. But I do load iron and have to have phlebotomies. I also learned that how I ate would have an impact on how often I had to donate blood. In the beginning I thought my mom was just being a typical mom when she kept reminding me to cut back on burgers and watch the high vitamin C drinks. After four years of learning how my body responds to iron and seeing for myself that I can control to some extent how much iron I absorb by watching what I eat, I now am more careful. When I ate mostly junk food and drank sodas or orange juice almost exclusively, I needed a phlebotomy more often. When I learned about iron bioavailability and how to block absorption I began cooking my own food. I changed the way I ate and found that I could go longer between phlebotomies. It is important to know that I don't drink alcohol or smoke, which can add to the problem. I now run at least two miles a day and feel great."

Jen's story: Jen found out that she was a compound heterozygote (two different mutations of the hemochromatosis gene HFE) after years of infertility, depression, and pain. Doctors told her hereditary hemochromatosis was rare and didn't affect females. Jen proved otherwise. She eventually received treatment (phlebotomy) and was deironed. She was now anemic but fearing her iron loading condition would cause the iron build back up, she decided that she wanted to reduce the amount of iron she consumed. Jen cut out all meat, wine, supplements, and vitamin C–rich foods and juices. To her surprise her ferritin levels began to drop as though she were having periodic phlebotomies. (It must be noted that persons with iron loading conditions whose tissue iron levels are very high, warranting phlebotomy, cannot efficiently reduce iron levels. In Jen's case, she was mildly anemic and her iron stores depleted as a result of blood removal. Jen soon learned by experimentation that she did not need such extreme diet changes.) Her maintenance needed balance in her diet. Jen began to include more iron-rich foods in her diet and her iron levels began to rise. She eventually needed another phlebotomy but has learned the importance of caution and balance in diet. "People can go to extreme," says Jen. "I did, because my doctors just didn't understand diet and iron overload. I think *Cooking with Less Iron* is an important book for anyone striving to keep iron levels in balance. Symptoms that resulted from my self-induced anemia were almost as bad as the symptoms of iron overload."

Cooking Tips

Health and safety:

Hot food should have a center temperature of 155 degrees, cold food a center temperature of 45 degrees.

White foods such as pasta and rice that are not properly cooled or fully reheated can provide the perfect environment for bacterial growth. All raw fruits and vegetables should be washed well before the skin is pierced. Melons, some berries, unpasteurized juices, and raw meat can contain E. coli bacteria. Handling of these foods then touching other foods without thoroughly washing one's hands can lead to cross contamination of this potentially deadly bacteria.

Use of antibacterial soaps is not necessary; any hand soap or mild bleach will clean a countertop sufficiently to sanitize it for use. Allow the countertop to dry completely before using.

Substitutions and the benefits of using brand name products:

My mother always stressed the importance of using established brand-name products. She felt that these products offered consistency in cooking and especially in baking. Over the years I have come to agree with her; I have tried substitutions only to be disappointed. Some of my favorite brand names include:

Berio (olive oil) Breakstone (sour cream, cottage cheese, ricotta), Breyers (frozen yogurt, ice cream, and ice milk), Dannon (yogurt), Folger's Coffee (instant and classic brew), Heinz (catsup and canned tomato products), Hellman's (mayonnaise), Jell-O (gelatins and puddings), Jif (peanut butter), Keebler (crackers), Kellogg's Complete Oat Bran, Kraft (cheeses and cheese products and some prepared salad dressings), Kikkoman (soy or teriyaki sauce), Lipton (tea), Nestle's and Hershey's (chocolate), Post Shredded Wheat Mini with Wheat Bran, Uncle Ben's (rice), Quaker Oats, and Ovaltine.

These products are used in the recipes contained in *Cooking with Less Iron* and are recommended for the best outcome.

Low fat tips and good substitutions:

Sour cream and mayonnaise are two fats that are prevalent in the American diet. In *Cooking with Less Iron,* sour cream especially is used in several recipes because of its iron-inhibiting characteristics. However, caution is offered with respect to the frequency one consumes these fats. Use of fat-free products offers some reduction in fat but often these products are high in sugar and sodium. One solution is to limit the number of times recipes with sour cream or mayonnaise are selected. Another approach is to use reduced fat products that you make yourself. Refer to reduced fat recipes such as mayonnaise, sour cream, bacon, and salad dressing (see the index).

Thickening agent: 1 tablespoon cornstarch = 2 tablespoons flour.

Vinegar: Substitute lemon juice.

Buttermilk = 1 cup sweet milk plus 1 tablespoon vinegar.

Table salt: No Salt by RCN Products or Morton's Lite Salt. Both products can leave a slightly bitter aftertaste when used in recipes that stand for a while. Lite Salt, was less bitter. Both taste fine in cooked or baked foods. Use these products as needed rather than using them in products prepared ahead.

Sugar substitute: Several varieties are available but they do not work well in cooked foods. Some will have a bitter after taste. Fructose is one product you can purchase through health food stores, but check with your physician if you have diabetes. Two products that can be cooked are Splenda and Alterna Sweet. Both work will in puddings, sauces, cheesecakes, pie filling and for general sweetening but neither work well in bakery items such as cakes. They are also more expensive than other sugar substitutes and sometimes more sweet than regular sugar but they appear to be safe for diabetics. You can read more about Splenda at www.splenda.com and Altera Sweet at www.alternasweet.com or call 888-668-8008.

Milk: Vitamite, nondairy beverage. This is a personal favorite of mine. I use it in my coffee and on cereal; it tastes just like milk to me. Anyone who is allergic to dairy might like to try this product. Vitamite cooks well, except that it will not thicken instant puddings. You will need to add 1 teaspoon of cornstarch dissolved in a bit of water to your instant pudding recipes if you use this nondairy product. If you cannot find Vitamite in stores call Diehl Products at 1-800-443-3930.

Equivalents:

3 teaspoons = 1 tablespoon

4 tablespoons = ¼ cup

5 tablespoons + 1 teaspoon = ⅓ cup

2 cups = 1 pint

2 pints = 1 quart

4 quarts = 1 gallon

1 ounce = 2 tablespoons

8 ounces = 1 cup

16 ounces = 1 pound

Glossary of Cooking Terms:

Bake: To cook in a covered or uncovered container in an oven.

Barbecue: To cook on a rack or grill over hot charcoal or gas flame.

Baste: To cover cooking food, usually meat, with liquid such as broth for the purpose of adding flavor or moisture.

Beat: To make a mixture of ingredients, such as cake batter, smooth by adding air using a wooden spoon, wire whisk, or electric mixer.

Blanch: To preheat or precook in boiling water or steam, usually for the purpose of canning or preserving a food item for long-term storage such as freezing or canning.

Blend: To combine two or more separate ingredients, such as oil and vinegar until they become one.

Boil: To cook in water or broth until bubbles rise rapidly to the surface. To bring to a rolling boil is to cook on high temperature until bubbles rise rapidly and continually.

Braise: To cook slowly in a small amount of liquid or in steam in a covered pan. Also referred to as fricassee.

Bread: To coat meat or vegetables such as eggplant with bread or cracker crumbs, usually after dredging in flour and egg or soaking in buttermilk then coating with bread crumbs.

Broil: To cook at a high temperature where heat source is from above, such as in an oven.

Chop: To cut into smaller pieces with a sharp knife or food processor.

Combine: To mix two or more ingredients.

Cream: To mix one or more ingredients such as sugar and butter together until soft and creamy.

Cut in: To distribute fat such as shortening or butter, usually into flour, using a fork or specialty tool called a pastry blender. This can also be accomplished with a food processor and some mixers.

Dice: To cut into small cubes.

Dissolve: To combine a dry substance and a liquid, resulting in a solution.

Dredge: To coat or sprinkle with flour or other fine substance such as sugar.

Fold: To combine gently, usually using a rubber spatula or wire whisk, with two motions. One motion cuts vertically through the mixture and the other turns the mixture over by sliding the implement across the bottom of the mixing bowl.

Fry: To cook in fat.

Grate: To reduce to small particles or short string-like pieces by scraping a food item on a hand-held grate, or in a food processor. Commonly used for cheeses or spices and to make hash brown potatoes.

Knead: To manipulate with a pressing, turning, folding, and stretching motion, usually by hand or with a special mixer attachment. This process is used mostly in bread-making.

Marinate: To allow food, usually meat, to stand in mixture of ingredients such as wine, herbs, honey, soy, etc., for a period of time, usually overnight so that added flavor can permeate food or to tenderize meat.

Mince: To cut or chop into small, fine pieces.

Mix: To combine two or more ingredients.

Parboil: To boil uncooked food until partially cooked, usually for the purpose of storage such as freezing.

Parch: To brown foods such as grains by means of dry heat.

Pasteurize : To preserve food, such as fruit juices, milk, and cheese, by heating to a temperature (140° to 180°F) that will destroy certain microorganisms and arrest fermentation.

Peel: To remove skins or the outer covering of fruits and vegetables.

Poach: To cook in hot water.

Puree: To force cooked food through a fine sieve, food mill, or to mix in a food processor, blender, or mixer until mixture is smooth and thick.

Reconstitute: To restore concentrated foods to their normal state, usually by adding water.

Reduce: To continue cooking a liquid until its volume is decreased, thickened or concentrated.

Rice: To force food through ricer, sieve, or food mill.

Roast: To cook by dry heat, usually in an oven in a roasting pan with a lid or in a roasting bag.

Sanitize: To clean with soap and water or bleach.

Sauté: To fry with a small amount of oil.

Sear: To brown meat quickly with intense heat.

Simmer: To cook in a liquid just below the boiling point.

Steam: To cook in a basket over hot, usually boiling water or in a pressure cooker.

Steep: To allow a substance, such as tea, to stand in liquid below the boiling point for the purpose of extracting flavor.

Sterilize: To destroy microorganisms usually with steam, dry heat, or by boiling in a liquid.

Stew: To cook slowly in a small amount of liquid.

Stir: To mix ingredients by hand, usually with a wooden spoon to avoid burning or to keep ingredients blended.

Tear: To pull apart by hand.

Whip: To rapidly beat air into foods such as eggs or heavy cream, to cause expansion.

Whisk: To combine ingredients, especially for sauces, with a wire whisk.

CONTACTS

For more information about hereditary hemochromatosis, iron overload, and other disorders of iron contact:

Iron Disorders Institute: 864-292-1175

Visit the website: www.irondisorders.org

Or write: Iron Disorders Institute, P.O. Box 2031, Greenville, SC 29602

Or ask for *Iron Disorders Institute Guide to Hemochromatosis* available in major bookstores

For more information about nutrition and diet visit the following websites:

http://arborcom.com/frame/arb_food.htm
http://sun.kent.wednet.edu/KSD/KR/APPLIED/HEALTH/nutrition_values.html
http://www.cdc.gov (search with words *nutrition* and *hemochromatosis)*
http://www.nal.usda.gov/fnic/foodcomp/
http://www.nih.gov (search with words *nutrition* and *hemochromatosis)*
http://www.nutritionfocus.com

Bibliography and Resources

Bendich, A. Calcium supplementation and iron status of females. *Nutrition* 2001 17:46–51.

Bothwell, T. H., Baynes, R. D., MacFarlane, B. J., MacPhail, A. P. Nutritional iron requirements and food iron absorption. *Journal of Internal Medicine* 1989, 226:357–365.

Cook, J. D., Monsen, E. R. Comparison of the effect of animal proteins on nonheme iron absorption. *American Journal of Clinical Nutrition* 1976, 29:859–867.

Cook, J. D., Reddy, M. B. Ascorbic acid has a pronounced enhancing effect on the absorption of dietary nonheme iron when assessed by feeding single meals to fasting subjects. *American Journal of Clinical Nutrition* 2001, 73:93–8.

Davidsson, L., Walczyk, T., Zavaleta, N., Hurrell, R. F. Improving iron absorption from a Peruvian school breakfast meal by adding ascorbic acid or Na(2)EDTA. *American Journal of Clinical Nutrition* 2001, 73:283–287.

Fleming, D. J., Jacques, P. F., Tucker, K. L., Massaro, J. M., D'Agostino, R. B., Sr, Wilson, P. W., Wood, R. J. Iron status of the free-living, elderly Framingham Heart Study cohort: an iron-replete population with a high prevalence of elevated iron stores. *American Journal of Clinical Nutrition* 2001, 73:638–646.

Garcia-Casal, M. N., Leets, I., Layrisse, M. Beta-carotene and inhibitors of iron absorption modify iron uptake by caco-2 cell. *Journal of Nutrition* 2000,130:5–9.

Hallberg,L., Hulthen, L. Prediction of Dietary Iron Absorption: An algorithm for calculating absorption and bioavailability of dietary iron. *American Journal of Clinical Nutrition* 2000, 71: 1147–1160.

Heath, A.L., Skeaff, C.M., Gibson, R.S. The relative validity of a computerized food frequency questionnaire for estimating intake of dietary iron and its absorption modifiers. *European Journal of Clinical Nutrition* 2000, 54:592–599.

Hunt, J. R., Roughead, Z. K. Nonheme iron absorption, fecal ferritin excretion, and blood indexes of iron status in women consuming controlled lactoovovegetarian diets for 8 weeks. *American Journal of Clinical Nutrition* 1999, 69: 944–952.

Hurrell, R. F., Reddy. M., Cook, J. D., Inhibition of non-haem iron absorption in man by polyphenolic-containing beverages. *British Journal of Nutrition* 1999, 81:289–295.

Hurrell, R. F., Reddy, M. B., Burri, J., Cook, J. D. An evaluation of EDTA compounds for iron fortification of cereal-based foods. *British Journal of Nutrition* 2000, 84:903–910.

Kamao, M., Tsugawa, N., Nakagawa, K., Kawamoto, Y., Fukui, K., Takamatsu, K., Kuwata, G., Imai, M., Okano, T. Absorption of calcium, magnesium, phosphorus, iron and zinc in growing male rats fed diets containing either phytate-free soybean protein or soybean protein isolate or casein. *Journal of Nutrition Science Vitaminol (Tokyo)* 2000, 46:34–41.

Kishida, T., Nakai, Y., Ebihara, K., Hydroxypropyl-distarch phosphate from tapioca starch reduces zinc and iron absorption, but not calcium and magnesium absorption, in rats. *Journal of Nutrition* 2001, 131:294–300.

Layrisse, M., Garcia-Casal, M., Solano, L., Baron, M., Arguello, F., Llovera, D., Ramierz, J., Leets, I. Tropper, E., Iron bioavailability in humans from breakfasts enriched with iron bis-glycine chelate, phytates and polyphenols. *Human Nutrition and Metabolism* 2000, 9: 2195–2199.

Levrat-Verny, M. A., Coudray, C., Bellanger, J., Lopez, H. W., Demigne, C., Rayssiguier, Y., Remesy, C. Wholewheat flour ensures higher mineral absorption and bioavailability than white wheat flour in rats *British Journal of Nutrition* 1999 82:17–21.

Morck, T. A., Lynch, S. R., Cook, J. D. Inhibition of Food Iron Absorption by Coffee. *The American Journal of Clinical Nutrition* 1983, 37:416–420.

Passwater, R.A., *All About Antioxidants*, Avery Publishing, Garden City Park, New York, 1998.

Roughead, Z. K., Hunt, J. R. Adaptation in iron absorption: iron supplementation reduces nonheme-iron but not heme-iron absorption from food. *American Journal of Clinical Nutrition* 2000, 72:982–989.

Sandstead, H. H. Causes of iron and zinc deficiencies and their effects on brain. *Journal of Nutrition* 2000,130:347S–349S.

Siegenberg, D., Baynes, R. D., Bothwell, T. H., MacFarlane, B. J., Lamparelli, R. D., Car, N. G., MacPhail, P., Schmidt, U., Tal, A., Mayet, F. Ascorbic acid prevents the dose-dependent inhibitory effects of polyphenols and phytates on nonheme-iron absorption. *American Journal of Clinical Nutrition* 1991, 53:537–541.

Zijp, I. M., Korver, O., Tijburg, L. B. Effect of tea and other dietary factors on iron absorption. *Critical Review Food Science & Nutrition* 2000, 40:371–398.

SUBJECT INDEX

Recipe Index